If Clutter Could Talk

The Stories It Would Tell

by Tracy Paye

Dear Leslie,

I hope this book heals your heart and brightens your life.

Best to you

Tracy

AKA Miss Organized

Editing - Laura Kwartler - www.writinginink.com
Cover Design - Lisa Smith - www.belladiadesign.com
Book Layout/Production - Cliff Durfee - www.designaffect.com
Publishing Consulting - Cliff Durfee - www.designaffect.com

If Clutter Could Talk: The Stories It Would Tell
by Tracy Paye
COPYRIGHT © 2013 by Tracy Paye
Published by Miss Organized - www.missorganized.com

Printed in the United States of America

LCCN 2013908697
ISBN 978-1-4848-2991-2

What People Say

"In my human experience the most compelling moments in my life, have come from someone helping me to expand my levels of self awareness. In this book, Tracy takes you by the hand through a journey of self awareness, which will inspire you to manifest your true self. Helping you to recognize and release the habits and thoughts that are no longer serving you, is the essence of this book."

Dulce Benetti

"Clutter isn't just about clutter; it is almost always an emotional journey. Using humor and poignant real life stories, Tracy gets to the heart of things. You may see yourself (or perhaps someone you know) in these stories. You can easily use the 'Take Aways' in each chapter to make improvements in your space and in your life. I highly recommend you read this great book or give it as a gift. If you are a coach, it will help you better understand what some of your clients may be dealing with, particularly when it comes to managing change."

Judy Peebles

International Speaker, Trainer, Business Strategist & Coach & Creator of The Journaling Jenius™, Journaling Jems™ and The Knowledge Series™

"Do you think an organizing book can't help you? That's what I thought as well. You know that saying, you don't know what you don't know? It's true, and this book helped me see the trail of what I was missing. Since I finished this book I started going to the gym and have begun to look at my clutter as my internal chaos exposed."

Jamie Grogan

"I initially thought: How interesting could this be? I expected this book would either be a boring technical approach to organization or a girly-girl chick book. What I've found was neither of these.

"Tracy has done a great job at explaining and comparing the causes of clutter, as well as making the subject entertaining and less intimidating. And, I appreciate her recognition that clutter is not as harmless as we might imagine, but can have a dramatic impact upon the productivity, relationships, and success in our life. You've done a great job here Tracy. I'm very impressed and have enjoyed the book. Well done!"

Stacy Silverwood
Artist & Photographer

"Well, I thought I was somewhat organized, but, after reading Tracy's book, I'm not! It inspired and motivated me to go THROUGH my closet and truly organize my clothes and shoes. Awesome book and an easy read that makes you WANT to get organized! Thank you Tracy ~ on to the next project!"

Elsa Petrick
Wellness Coach & Nutritionist

"I have always wondered why I can't "just get it together" and thought it's just a personal weakness. After reading Tracy's book, I know I am not alone, and better yet—there is help for people like me!

"This book works great for me since it is a series of short stories; each that can easily be read in a matter of minutes. Her writing is funny and insightful at the same time, and Tracy makes you feel like you are right there living these scenes with her. Within the humor though is the true compassion Tracy obviously feels for her clients and the struggles they go through.

"I realized that if I want to solve my clutter issues, I need to treat them as seriously as someone who hires a personal exercise trainer. Professional Organizers, like Tracy, have special skill sets to help those of us who need coaching on how to get out of the stranglehold of clutter."

Jennifer Ables
Style Consultant with J. Hilburn Men's Clothier

Acknowledgements

To my clients for trusting me to come into your lives and your home, for finding the courage to take action, and inspiring me to continue to do what I do with your amazing stories of transformation.

To my support system who believed in me, encouraged me to be the best I can be, pushed me to be even better, and never let me have a pity party for too long.

To Mark LeBlanc for urging me to write this book and having the confidence in me that I could.

To the people on the show "Mission Organization" on HGTV, from whom I learned that organizing was a profession and it was the perfect fit for me.

To my client in the Stranger Danger story who passed away on May 24, 2012. Thank you for giving me an opportunity to write your story and share it with the world. You will be dearly missed.

To my amazingly creative book cover designer Lisa Smith of Belladia Design who always brilliantly brings my ideas to life.

To my inside-book-layout production designer, publishing consultant, and long time friend, Cliff Durfee, who has been there with me from the beginning of Miss Organized and has provided an incredible amount of love, support, and direction in my life and my business.

To Laura Kwartler, client, friend, and content editor of this book. Thank you Laura for creating structure and organization around my thoughts and providing positive and constructive feedback along the way.

To my mom who modeled a deep compassion for helping those in need and working incredibly hard to keep a clean home.

To my dad for passing on his natural gift of organizing and always allowing me to be me.

Foreword
by Mark LeBlanc, Small Business Success
Author of *Growing Your Business!* and, *Never Be the Same*

What is it about getting organized that so many of us resist? When we do take some steps towards that end, it feels so good, so why don't we make the commitment to really get organized once and for all? Secondly, what if we then made it a habit to maintain that organization on a regular basis?

Yes, if only clutter could talk? What would clutter say? Clutter would urge you to call Little Miss Organized, Tracy Paye. Tracy is one of those rare people who come into your life, shake it up and you will never be the same after. I think the energizer bunny was modeled after Tracy.

She has captured the essence of what it means to live an organized life, and create an environment that supports your work, dreams, and goals. Not only does she provide you with what you need to know, she provides you with what you need to do and in many cases will work side-by-side with you to get the job done, whatever it takes!

This gem of a book contains the wisdom, strategies, and ideas you want, and can make a big difference in how you live your life. It will put you in a position to help you reach more of your potential and have fun doing it. Her enthusiasm is infectious, and her commitment to helping others is clearly evident, like a pitbull tearing into a piece of prime beef.

The best piece of advice I can give you is to devour this book. Keep it within arm's reach and refer to it often. Take action on what you learn and let the humor contained in this book inspire you to keep it together when it gets messy all over again. Start reading now, and you will find out how simple this can be, and how fast you can experience the results of being organized. And we all know that an organized life, is a fun life.

Introduction

Have you ever made the effort to get organized, only to find your space quickly getting disorganized again? Do you have trouble letting things go, and don't know why? Are you willing yourself into getting organized only to find you can't get started or complete the project? Are you overwhelmed with anxiety the minute you walk into your home or office?

If you are like most of my clients, trying to get organized is something you have been struggling with for years. You've read how-to get organized books, cut out magazine articles with the latest organizing tools and products, set aside time in your schedule to organize, watched organizing techniques on organizing shows, bought storage containers, and maybe even moved into a bigger space in hopes that it will be the magic cure to solve your problems with clutter and disorganization. But no matter what you do, you still aren't getting and staying organized. After three decades of helping people in their homes and offices to get organized, I have discovered why this is and I have found applying my insight to help people to be infinitely rewarding.

In my role of Certified Professional Organizer, I have found myself acting as a life coach, cheerleader, health and wellness advisor, business consultant, and even a marriage and family counselor. Several times, I've played mediator between husbands and wives, or parents and children when blow ups, meltdowns, and communication breakdowns occur. It has proven to be an eye-opener for me, as well as my clients, leading to the undeniable knowledge that issues involving disorganization and clutter go far deeper than finding the time to organize, getting a bigger space, purchasing the right containers, or applying the latest tips and techniques. As a result, I long ago incorporated the study of human behavior and emotions into my repertoire; something that

I have found to be fascinating, as well as useful.

What I realized during my three decades in this profession is that at the core of most clutter problems is an emotional attachment to the very things that are causing the client such distress. Along with giving me access to their spaces and the physical possessions within them, clients have also shared with me their life stories. These stories were filled with fear, anger, resentment, disappointment, regret, hate, and all sorts of negative emotions that got in the way of their ability to make healthy decisions about their stuff. My job is a very intimate one, and it's not just because I actually have to go into someone's underwear drawer to get it done. Clients have confessed their secrets, wishes, fears, frustrations, and the problems they have faced. This still occurs today and I know to listen for those cues.

Much of the knowledge that I use to help my clients has come from not just studying cutting-edge organizational techniques, but also from studying and observing human emotions and behaviors, my experience working with clients, instinct, intuition, and a large dose of self exploration. It is this combination that I use to not only organize people's spaces, but help them to better understand themselves, their environments, their situations, and the other people in their lives. There is nothing I love more than when I give an explanation as to why someone does what they do and are who they are and they look at me with a surprised and liberated look on their face and say, "You hit the nail on the head!"

This book is filled with stories of my client's own struggles with clutter and disorganization, the emotions we discovered at the core of those struggles, what we did to overcome them, and what happened in their lives as a result. You'll be shown that once we, my client and I working together, have uncovered the emotion that was creating the attachment to their things, they come to see the emotional heaviness they have been carrying around and the impact it has had on their life – not just in their clutter surroundings, but in their closest personal relationships – and start to let it all go. Once this starts, they gain the freedom and confidence to move out of indecision and feeling stuck, to taking action, moving forward, and having massive breakthroughs that resulted in inspiring internal and external transformations. Once they have a taste of this, they are motivated and determined to keep going, never wanting to go back to the way things were.

Hopefully, while reading this book, you see similarities to your own experiences, realize you are not alone, and understand that there is most always an unconscious reason for your clutter. I hope you will find the courage to look for the emotional attachment you may be having to your things and gain the willingness to create a new story, and the motivation to take action so you too can loosen your grip on what doesn't work in your life, attract what does, and create a less stressful and more enjoyable life.

Embedded in the stories, you will also find organizing strategies, techniques, and tips, like how to help your kids clean their rooms easier, how to organize clothes in a closet, rearranging furniture, and changing the function of a room to better suit your needs.

Along with this information, I've also included a few simple exercises you can do to help increase your ability to take action and create awareness around your emotions. I've also included advice on how to select and work with a Professional Organizer.

Finally, at the end of this book I've listed some helpful resources you can check out, including where to read my blog where I share more stories and techniques and how you can contact me if you have any additional questions.

About the Author

It started when I was twelve. Ellen wanted to play; I wanted to organize her room for her. Twenty-five years later, I finally realized why she stopped inviting me over to play. Since I was twelve, I've developed a lifelong passion and fascination with creating order and clarity out of chaos. Restoring calm and unleashing maximum potential within spaces, people, and businesses brings me joy.

Miss Organized Professional Organizing Services was born six months after I learned that organizing was a profession made for me, and since 2003, I have been transforming homes and offices into comfortable, convenient, and productive spaces. My mission is to help people clear their mess to relieve their stress so they can thrive instead of merely survive.

To learn more about Tracy Paye and her services in the San Diego, CA area, visit her website at www.tracypaye.com

Dedication

To my funny, incredibly smart, and outrageously vivacious redheaded daughter who motivates me to clear out my own internal clutter and to be the best role model I can be for her and her future children. I love you with all my heart and soul, Paris.

Table of Contents

Chapters

"I'm not sure I need 67 pencil sharpeners but you never know when that Army of pencils will show up."

Client Quote

"Because of you I don't have to take a Xanax every time I come into this room."

Client Quote

"Think about any attachments that are depleting your emotional reserves. Consider letting them go."

Oprah Winfrey

"Three Rules of Work: Out of clutter find simplicity. From discord find harmony. In the middle of difficulty lies opportunity."

Albert Einstein

chapter 1

The Snake Lady

Chapter 1

The client

When she finally called me, Jennifer was a single, divorced mom living with her ten year-old son Zack. Jennifer is a school teacher on her summer break when she decided to do something about the clutter that had taken over her dining and living rooms. Uncertain whether it was the right course of action, but not knowing what else to do, she called me and said that she just couldn't take another moment living the way she was - embarrassed to have people over.

Unlike many of my clients who just say they want to get better organized, Jennifer had a clear understanding of the impact of living in a disorganized space had on her life. During our first telephone call she told me that she had woken up one day and saw how she was shutting people out of her life, other than her boyfriend, and that her home was uninviting and lonely. She wanted out of the hermit life and wanted to start entertaining in her home.

What's up with that?

Clutter is often an unconscious statement to the world that someone is shutting off from the inside out. This can happen when people get into a place in their lives they are ashamed of who they have become or disappointed in what they have failed to achieve, or both. Depending on the depth of the unconscious feelings, clutter can manifest itself as more than just too much stuff, but can actually manifest as unsafe living conditions. Then, hopefully, one day the silent sufferer wakes up and sees the clutter around them, and though they may not have fully realized the connection between their clutter and the state of their lives or emotions, I get what I call the "911 plea." It goes something like this:

> *Hi, my name is so and so and I am totally overwhelmed. I have been living like this for a while and I can't handle it anymore. Help me Obi Wan Kenobi you're my only hope. Can you get here yesterday?*

At least half of the emails I receive have "HELP!!!!" in the subject line.

I sum up this sequence into three phases that I call "The Three A's," they are: (1) **A**wareness, (2) **A**cceptance, and (3) **A**ction.

The first, the *Awareness phase,* is when someone realizes that all their attempts to conquer their clutter on their own prove to not hold up over the long run.

Phase two is the *Acceptance phase.* This happens when a *clutterer* accepts that they need help and are open to accepting help. Hopefully they don't get stuck in this phase and decide to move into the action phase. This is when they finally feel ready to make the commitment to get their space organized and have become willing to do what it takes to make the changes they need to make, *no matter what.* This is when I and other Professional Organizers often receive the call for "HELP!"

In the third phase, the *Action phase,* that's when the real work begins. Stuff begins to get sorted, emotions get uncovered, strategies that fit the person's actual life are created, and, ultimately, things and emotional baggage are gotten rid of. Sometimes, it's not until frustration sets in during this phase, that the call will go out.

It would save a person a lot of time, money, energy, and suffering if they didn't wait till their lives fell apart before they reached out for help. But I know that for many of my clients, that was what it took before they were willing to change and accept the help.

The assessment

When I entered Jennifer's home the first thing she told me was how embarrassed she was to have me see her place and to invite anyone over. This reaction is pretty common. One of the things she was most embarrassed about was the dog pee stains on the carpet in the dining room and the obvious smell emanating from it.

Rather than using the dining room for entertaining the guests she was missing from her life, it was being used as her son's play/work area where he built model toy cars. The space was un-inviting, dark, messy, and disorganized. I couldn't imagine how he even could successfully build a model in this space.

She then showed me that the dining room table was placed in the eat-in kitchen. In this space her son's toys were also scattered about.

After the walk-through, Jennifer and I sat down to talk through what she thought her space needed and my initial impressions. She told me that the only solution she could see to making her home more inviting was to move all of her son's toys up to his bedroom and return the kitchen and dining room to their intended use. Instinctively, I did not think this was a good idea, but continued to listen and ask questions.

When I asked her where she spent the majority of her time, I was not surprised when she told me it was in the kitchen. This is usually the most high traffic area in a home. When I looked at the eat in kitchen and I saw that some of Zack's toys and model parts had migrated into that area, I immediately got a sense that he was doing this because he was uncomfortable being in the dining room alone. This may have also explained why he didn't keep the dining room area, his designated play area, clean. I've noticed that when people don't feel comfortable in a space, they aren't as motivated to stay in it, let alone keep it clean and organized. I also sensed that his parents divorce was causing him to feel a greater need to be in closer proximity to wherever his mother was in the house.

That this was the room where there were dog pee stains in the carpet also added to Zack's discomfort. While kids tend to be messier than adults, feeling disconnected in a space and acting out on it can also apply to them and I thought that it did in this case. I shared my thoughts with her and we came up with an initial action plan.

The change — action phase

The first actions I suggested we take was to move the dining room table into the dining area and make the eat-in kitchen a workspace for handling the household paperwork, as well as a place for her son to build his models with his mother close by.

Jennifer, however, was hesitant to make the switch right then because of the stained and smelly carpet in the dining area. She told me she wanted to rip it up first, so, knowing that waiting was procrastination and that would not serve the client, I looked at her and asked "What about now?" Shocked and nervous, she readily agreed.

With knives in hand, we laughed as we ripped up the carpet and cut it into manageable pieces. Then, looking like we were carrying a dead body, we carted the rolled up pieces to the dumpster, and that was that. The cement under the carpet actually looked better than the carpet had been looking for a while.

We set up the new dining area by pulling in some pieces from the other rooms and gave it an Asian style look.

In the eat-in kitchen, we used plastic drawers we had purchased to create her son's workspace area and divided up all the model parts. We also set up her filing system so she could easily find and put away her paperwork.

Once those major areas were complete, she felt good about now being in a space where she would feel comfortable inviting people over. She was excited to move on to other rooms and we tackled the living room next.

We re-designed her living room by applying Feng Shui principles to create greater flow of energy in the arrangement of the existing furniture. When we were done, the space was conducive to guests moving around and being able to converse from their seated position.

While Jennifer left to pick up her son and bring him home, I neatened all the wires and game boxes of Zack's video game collection so that the entertainment armoire doors could now close instead of being held open by wires. When Jennifer returned she actually did the hands to the face expression and exclaimed "Oh my God." That's the reaction us Organizers live for. It's the juice for my batteries and inspires me to do what I do.

Still energized and having fun, Jennifer had us tackle her guest room where we set up a crafting area for her hobby. Something she had never done for herself before.

Mom boundaries

Let's talk about "mom boundaries" for a second. As moms, we have a tendency to take care of everyone else's needs first without sometimes nurturing our own. One of the simplest ways you can nurture the other parts of yourself that existed before mommyhood took over is to create a space of your own in your home. Even if it's a small area, you need to have a space where no one can touch your stuff, or put their things. A place you have full control over how it looks and feels. Set this up for yourself, and just watch what a difference it makes in your well-being and mommy patience.

Exercise: Create your sacred space

Whether it's just a corner of a room or a full on mom cave, carve out a piece of real estate just for you where you have total say over what it looks and feels like. Whether it's a place to express your inner genius, connect with nature or just sit and relax, make this a space that inspires the feeling or state of mind you want to achieve when you are in it. Here are some examples of sacred spaces you can create:

- A small section of your kitchen countertop turned into an efficient workspace area to process papers without interruption
- A mani/pedi area equipped with a comfy chair and relaxing music
- A workout area to do yoga, weight training or Zumba
- A vanity area all chicked out that makes you feel sexy and beautiful when getting ready
- A bench in your backyard to sit and write
- A wall to hang your favorite piece of art

It's important when creating this area that you snazz it up so that it is not only visually appealing, but also comfortable and easy to use. Colors, art, music, candles, cozy blankets and scenic views will all add to the ambience and increase your desire to keep it sacred. Set this up for yourself, and just watch what a difference it makes in your state of mind and ability to care for the ones you love.

Back to the action

During the day of organization, we had set aside the items Jennifer was going to donate to charity. The plan was to have her boyfriend take these items to a donation center, but when she asked him to she discovered he was resistant to performing this task. As we talked about it, we both realized that he was fearful of her "straightening" her life out because it made him wonder what would that mean for him. Would she "purge" him too, he wondered, presciently as it ultimately turned out.

When your support system doesn't support you

When you decide to get organized, you may find that the people in your life may not support you. This has nothing to do with you or even how they feel about you. Change can be scary for anyone. It makes them wonder about their place in your life. You will have to find the courage to not let this stop you. One way to do this is by not forcing the changes you're making in your space or your mutual home on their personal spaces. When you put the focus on taking care of your stuff, without getting on other people about theirs, they will see the positive effect it's having on you and want some of the new-found *mojo* you're experiencing. They'll notice a difference in you, and that just might cause a difference in them. You just may find by starting to de-clutter even a small little space that it will create an energy that motivates the others in your home to get organized too.

Turning lemons into lemonade

I'm a firm believer in life being guided by the energy you put out. I also subscribe to the the *Feng Shui* principle that everything is energy. Organizing doesn't just move stuff, it also moves energy that has been stuck for a while. I often find that disturbing this energy can lead to strange results. Such was the case with Jennifer's home. Within a week of getting organized, the pipes in her upstairs bathroom burst, requiring the bathroom floor to be ripped up. It caused complete chaos in her life for about a week.

You're probably asking right now, "Well then why in the heck would I want to get organized and use Feng Shui if something negative might happen?" The answer is simply that often times in order to bring in the new you have to get rid of the old. The negative experience will turn into an experience that will eventually serve your life in a very positive way. Think about how many times something bad happened, that wound up being a blessing in disguise because of the good that came from it. For this reason, de-cluttering can be considered creative destruction. Jennifer's burst pipes crisis became a make lemonade out of lemons situation.

It turned out she had wanted to replace the bathroom floor for some time, but didn't have the money to do so. Because of what appears to have originally been a "bad thing," she was able to get her homeowner's insurance to pay to replace the bathroom floor with very little out of pocket expense from her. Sweet deal right?

Another change that happened in her life was that she decided to let go of her boyfriend. When I contacted her two years later to let her know I was going to write about her story in this book, she told me, "I ended that relationship a year ago. Good guy, but still keeping his fourth grade essays stored in his garage, along with so many other things. Until I met you, that seemed quirky and kinda cute. It took a while for me to see it for what it was: an inability or unwillingness to let go of the past and move forward in life. Needless to say, our relationship wasn't moving forward either."

Like so many of my clients, the organizing process opened her eyes to help her see that not only was there a pile up of physical stuff in her life that wasn't serving her, but neither were some of the people. People can be clutter too. Get organized and watch the dynamics between you and the people in your life change, though usually for the better. This is not to say that people who start out unsupportive, or who are not similarly inspired to clean up their act have to be jettisoned from your life. That is not the purpose or intent of this kind of work, this is and should be about you and your personal space. For Jennifer, however, looking at her boyfriend's clutter illustrated that the relationship would never grow to where she needed it to go, because his clutter and unsupportive behavior was an illustration of his emotional limitations. In my experience, relationships of all kinds usually improve exponentially once the client removes their barriers and it proves to be a positive inspiration. Such was the case for Jennifer with her son, she became more aware of her choices and mistakes as a mother and the steps she needed to take to be an even better mother.

During our follow-up call, Jennifer was also proud to say that two years after the process, the dining room and living room had remained organized and justifiably bragged that it looked "beautiful." Her son's new play space she admitted, however, had become disorganized again. She acknowledged that she was aware that she had allowed him to "take over much of the lower level with all his model car stuff, and that's a problem." In our discussion I reminded her of what she already knew, that both organization and motherhood is about progress, not perfection, and that both are something you have to work at every day. Just as Jennifer had to train herself in new behaviors, she also had to do the same with her son. Now that she had internalized how she had contributed to the clutter and had modified her behavior, she could recognize her son's contribution to the mess and continue to work with him to set boundaries and take on habits that would help him for the rest of his life.

Why do I call Jennifer the Snake Lady?

I know the suspense is killing you and you're wondering why I titled this chapter "The Snake lady." Well, Jennifer waited until after I was done and gone to share that her son's 4-ft long snake had somehow managed to escape while I was in the house. She chose not to tell me at the time because she thought I might freak out. Well, she was RIGHT! I hate snakes. Seriously, I will sometimes wake up in a cold sweat when I have a dream with snakes in it.

They found the thing had slithered its way into a tool box and was just waiting for the poor fool to open it up so it could sink its 10-inch fangs into their neck.

Ok, that's probably not what would have happened, but in my mind that's totally what would have happened.

The Snake Lady TAKE AWAYS

1. Clutter can cause and be caused by negative feelings, including embarrassment, which in turn could cause someone to shut people out of their life by cluttering up their home.

2. Children going through change, like a divorce, will feel more comfortable in their play/work spaces if they are in close

proximity to their parents. The more comfortable someone is in their space, the more likely they are to want to stay in it, keep it clean and organized.

3. When you have moved through the 2 A's, the phases of *Awareness* and *Acceptance*, chances are you will be more ready and willing to move into the 3rd phase, which is taking *Action* to change your clutter situation.

4. Creating your own nurturing space within your home is a form of setting boundaries, which is essential for your well-being, and, therefore, that of anyone that you care for.

5. Moving energy can sometimes cause things to fall apart in your life because what is not serving you will go out and allow the new and better to come in.

~ ~ ~ ~ ~ ~ ~ ~

"The only things that can get into the garage are dwarfs and very thin dwarfs."

Client Quote

"I once had Feng Shui but I killed it. My Feng went Shui."

Client Quote

"More important than learning how to recall things is finding ways to forget things that are cluttering the mind."

Eric Butterworth

Just For Now

Chapter 2

The client

Margaret was a military wife and nurse who emailed me one of those panicked 911 emails that she needed to get her entire townhome in order before her husband returned from deployment. She was clearly overwhelmed and when I asked her when she wanted to get started she boldly exclaimed, "Yesterday!"

A seemingly upbeat and confident woman, Margaret turned out to be one of my most interesting clients. In our emails, Margaret revealed to me that, although not officially diagnosed, she believed she has Attention Deficit Hyperactivity Disorder (ADHD) and that was why she could not keep her new townhome organized. Margaret was diagnosed with clinical depression, so it did not seem unlikely to me that she could also suffer from ADHD.

ADHD and disorganization

It's a well documented fact that people who suffer from ADHD do have a harder time keeping their space clutter-free and organized than those who don't. It's especially challenging for those ADHD sufferers who are also diagnosed with depression: a dual diagnosis that is very common. Sufferers of ADHD can especially benefit from a Professional Organizer who implements systems that cater specifically to the strengths and methods that the client can maintain.

The assessment

During our initial consultation, Margaret revealed that this townhome was the first place her and her husband had owned. Because of her husband's service in the military throughout their marriage, they had moved frequently and lived in temporary military housing. She was, to her surprise, feeling uncomfortable setting up a permanent home, especially without his input. It was easy for me to recognize that, as a consequence of moving around, it was difficult for Margaret to feel grounded in whatever place she was calling home because every time she would start to feel like she was growing roots, she would get plucked up and planted somewhere else. This led her to live in places with a "just for now" mentality, a mentality that makes one resistant to turning a space into a home.

Snazz up your "just for now" space

When someone is bouncing around in their living situations, it tends to create a state of mind that says, "I'm just here for now." I can tell when someone has this self talk going on because they commonly use words like "someday" "when" or "just for now" in discussions about how they would like their home to look. I can also tell if someone is living in a temporary state of mind by the furniture they choose and how they set it in place. The lack of decorative touches like colorless walls and the absence of wall art or pictures of friends and family is also an indicator of a "just for now" mindset.

What I work to get across to clients, is that just because you decide to paint, buy a new piece of furniture, or move things around doesn't mean you will be stuck where you are forever. Nor should you resist doing those things just because a place is temporary. It is okay, in fact healthy, for you to be okay with where you are now. It makes it a lot easier to get to that future you dream about.

Back to the assessment

Now, had you walked into her place, most people would not have thought it to be that disorganized. This surprised me given the emails we had exchanged, but I have enough training and experience to know that disorganization and clutter is relative to how the person who lives in it perceives what an organized space should look like.

The first area I saw was the living room. Although the furniture placement made it look cold, and it could have been functionally set up better, it didn't look particularly cluttered.

My impression about the home changed when we made our way up into the upstairs office, which incidentally is where the prosperity area sits in some Feng Shui methodologies. I walked in and KABOOM! It looked like a bomb went off. There were papers everywhere and you had to walk over things just to get to the desk. Not what I was expecting after seeing the entryway and living room areas.

Although Margaret maintained a bubbly, fun, and upbeat attitude through the assessment, her clutter was showing me the truth of how she really felt inside.

What clutter is trying to say

I believe clutter is simply feelings unconsciously expressed. It's says, "Look at how depressed I am" or "I don't care about myself and no one cares about me." It can manifest in an entire home, or it can be limited to a single space. Sometimes the "where" also sends a message, but sometimes it's just a convenient space for the unconscious feelings to express themselves.

For Margaret, the state of her home was overwhelming to her, not just in the office, but also the disconnectedness she felt in the living areas. It fed into her depression and the ADHD she felt she had, and caused her a great deal of stress that she covered over with the bold confidence she used to get through the day.

The change - action phase

The living room was the first place of attack. With a kitty corner here, a moving of a bookcase there, and a smidge of decorative accents, even I was shocked at how fabulous this room turned out. We also took the couch and brought it closer to the center of the room and angled it. She was totally open to the changes and loved how much cozier her living room felt and looked once we were done.

You wouldn't believe how nervous angling a couch makes some people feel. They have known no other way to place their furniture, except for pushed up against a wall. News flash! Kitty cornering is in! It's delightfully rebellious. Try it. You might be surprised how making this simple change can give a room a totally different look and feel. Plus, you could wind up creating a storage space behind the furniture that you may not have otherwise had.

After having fun with all the creativity, space re-design, and decorating in the living room, we then suited up and prepared for battle in the paper warzone that was her office.

As I do for every project, I dug into her office by starting with the first step of getting organized which is sorting. Sorting happens by collecting the items in the space and grouping them into categories with other items that are similar in the function they perform. For example, scissors, a letter opener, and a razor blade are all things that cut. By remembering the function an item performs, and grouping it with items that perform that or a similar function, it will be easier and faster for you to find what you are looking for because you won't have to remember where each and every item is.

Technique: Stressed, Stop, and Sort™

It is imperative for the completion of your project, or at least moving a project forward, that you work on it in steps. Applying a step-by-step approach will help you move through an organizing project more efficiently, while at the same time reducing the amount of overwhelm and frustration most people experience when they attempt to get organized on their own. In fact, spending a few moments sorting your stuff when you feel overwhelmed is a simple, easy, and fast way to relieve stress instantly. I've trained my clients to remember a technique I call, Stressed, Stop, and Sort™. For this technique I recommend you have the following supplies on hand.

SUPPLIES:
>3-10 cardboard bankers boxes
>Bach's Rescue Remedy or herbal tea

Exercise: Practice Stressed, Stop, And Sort™

1. When you feel yourself starting to get stressed out, first stop what you are doing, or at least give yourself fifteen minutes of transition time to stop what you are doing. For additional help to calm yourself down, I recommend using Bach's Rescue Remedy and taking a few deep breaths or having a cup of herbal tea, or whatever you typically use to calm you down.

2. After you've stopped what you are doing and calmed down a bit, get the boxes and set them on the floor to get ready for sorting. To prevent overwhelm and blocking your walkways with boxes, I highly recommend placing them in a straight line, about five across. A couple rows may be necessary. Doing it this way will help the process go much faster and feel a lot easier.

3. Lastly, look around the immediate space you are in and ask yourself the question: what can you easily sort, within fifteen minutes in to the following three categories?

   a. What belongs in the current room
   b. What belongs in another room
   c. Paper

You can always micro-sort the categories even further if you have the time, energy, and focus to do so at that moment, but sorting into bigger categories at first is a start, and will help you to see clear spaces faster.

For this strategy to effectively work, you need to make sure that those items have a home to go in to, and that you are putting those things back into their designated homes within the next three days. Otherwise, they will continue to sit in the containers and stress you out. This technique works really well at desks when a flurry of activity can leave your desktop cluttered in a short period of time with paper and other random items. Using this technique will help you to immediately see clear spaces, which will help clear your mind, lower your stress, as well as increase your focus and productivity.

Find in five seconds with *Paper Tiger*

After we separated items into like categories and then did the next step, saying adios to what she no longer needed, we had to find a system for her to use in the fourth step, which is to contain her items into a storage unit.

When deciding what to do with her papers, I knew just using a filing cabinet to contain her documents would not work for Margaret, so I introduced her to a couple different document management systems. The first one, a desktop program and web application, called *Paper Tiger* guarantees you will find your documents in five seconds or less by eliminating the errors, confusion, and frustration that typically occur when people try to file into or access documents from a filing system.

Many times, traditional filing systems stored in a file cabinet become a disorganized nightmare, especially if more than one person is accessing those documents. It relies on remembering what you named a document and where you filed it, as well as routine purging so the file drawer doesn't get crammed with papers.

Paper Tiger works by using any number of keywords or "tags" to identify a document so it can be easily found later. For instance, if you want to file an auto registration, you can tag it with the word auto or registration or even the make of the car, like Honda. When you go to look for it again, and you forget what you named the file or where you put it, you can use *Paper Tiger* to find it under any one of those keywords. It even has a feature that alerts you when it's time to purge a document so you don't wind up with overflowing files. Check the resource list at the end of this book to get more information on *Paper Tiger*.

I also showed her File Solutions, a document management system that uses pre-designed, color-coded labels to put on file folders for filing papers away into a filing cabinet or file box. She loved the colors of File Solutions and how it already came with pre-determined categories. She also liked that using *Paper Tiger*, helped her to find her documents even faster, so she decided to combine the two.

Two years later, she reported to me that she was still successfully managing her documents using both systems and that she felt more in control and that a huge weight had been lifted from her shoulders, instilling a greater sense of hope and clarity. That's what I aim for with my all my clients.

Match your system with the way you think

One of the biggest mistakes people make when determining what system or tools would be best to manage their time, paper, emails, tasks, and projects is choosing a system or tools that don't work with the way they think. For example, visual thinkers also tend to be creative-types. This is why using systems that are visually appealing will make them feel more motivated to want to stick with it. If they don't like the way it looks, it will be harder for them to want to keep using it.

File folders come in all sorts of fun colors and designs now. You can get them at just about any place that sells office supplies. I actually use hot pink and black folders from the Container Store, which are the same colors I use in my brand. Looking at my pretty business folders, makes me feel very Carrie from Sex and the City, and creates the perfect vibe for when I feel like sitting down to write.

Sometimes, the information needs to be right in front of the visual organizer, or the size of the paper needs to be bigger for them to efficiently process the information. They may prefer to see their schedule on a color-coded calendar, rather than written in pencil on a planner.

If you know that you work better writing things down on paper, instead of putting it in your computer, then a digitally based system, no matter how rad it is, may not work for you. Or maybe you're like me and use both paper and digital systems depending on the type of information you're managing. Pay attention to yourself and how you operate to see if you can notice what information organization works better for you. Once you become aware of your digital or paper preference, you then need to ask yourself the following questions:

1. Is my information easy to store away?
2. Can I find it quickly when I need to?
3. Can I easily take action on the information when I'm ready to?

If you can't answer "yes" to all those questions, something within the systems you are using to store your information needs to change, or a whole new system needs to be created all together.

Having the inability to store and retrieve your information easily and quickly could be due to the fact that some of the information you need access to while on the go is located at your home or office. This would make doing activities like calling the hot lead while you were on the road difficult because you may not have the information with you while you are traveling. In that case a paper planner, like the Franklin Planner, would be a good way for you to write your information down and carry it with you on the go.

Chapter 2

If you really want to be an organized ninja, you would consider putting the contact information on your smartphone instead. At first, you may still feel the urge to write it down on a piece of paper. That's okay. It will take some time to break you of this habit, but if you consistently practice immediately putting contact information into your phone, you will save yourself the time and hassle of having to look for where you wrote down the information later and potentially miss the opportunity to acquire a new client. If productivity and efficiency are important to you, I highly recommend you get a smartphone, if you don't already have one. I don't know how I would manage half the things I have to do in my life without my iPhone. It's a life saver.

Finding a system that matches the way you think and operate is vital to your peace and productivity. Once you know how you work, and accept this about yourself, it will be easier to find the system that works best for you and stick with it.

Saved from disaster

During the organizing process, Margaret's water heater broke. As a result, she learned when she bought her home she did not purchase the homeowner's warranty insurance that would have paid for its replacement. We both agreed that this minor problem was a blessing in disguise because it alerted her to the fact that she did not have the home owner's insurance she thought she had and had it been another problem that caused a lot of damage it would have been financially devastating. As a good counterpoint, while we were going through some of her paperwork in her office, we found a total of $6,000 worth of checks she had lost and still needed to deposit.

It is surprising to me how often I find lost money with clients. It's not unusual for me to have clients pay me with money that we found during a project. I actually had a woman pay me with all the money she had in a Winnie the Pooh bank she got from Tijuana. I took it to a Coinstar to cash it in and, I'm not kidding, I sat at that machine for 30 minutes. It was like Vegas in Vons and it attracted a crowd. When the bling bling of the machine was done, it totaled up to be over $600 worth of coins.

Just For Now TAKE AWAYS

1. Any person, especially people suffering from ADHD can benefit from implementing systems that match their strengths with methods they can maintain. If you can't figure it out for yourself, an experienced and Certified Professional Organizer will save you a lot of time and money by helping you decide which systems would work best for you.

2. Clutter is emotions unconsciously expressed and can manifest in an entire home or be limited to a single space. Regardless, it is communicating emotions that a clutterer may or may not be vocally expressing.

3. Even if you are in a space "just for now" you can still snazz it up so it's comfortable and enjoyable for the time you are there. Being okay with and making the most of where you are at now, will make it a lot easier to get to the future you dream about.

4. When you feel yourself getting stressed out in your space, use the Stressed, Stop, and Sort™ strategy to clear your space and clear your mind.

5. *Paper Tiger* and File Solutions are two great systems to help find your documents faster and easier.

6. Know thy self to understand if using a paper or a digital based system to manage your information works best for you. Storing your information in an area that you can access

easily when you are away from your home or office may be the change you need to make in order to manage the information more efficiently.

7. To determine if the systems you are using to manage your information are working for you, ask yourself if you can:
   a. Store your information away easily
   b. Find it quickly when you need to
   c. Easily take action on the information when you are ready to

8. You never know what you'll find in clutter.

Husband, *"I'm surrendering. Whatever you say to do Tracy I will do."*

Client Quote

"We have enough Triscuits for a nuclear holocaust."

Client Quote

"There came a day when I had to say goodbye to the purple satin disco pants. It was a sad day."

Client Quote

"If you look at your entire house as one unit of junk, you'll never do anything because the job is too overwhelming. Take it one drawer at a time."

Janet Luhrs

"Life is really simple, but we insist on making it complicated."

Confucius (Chinese philosopher)

Chapter 3

Diapers, Toothpicks, and Bread Clips, Oh My!

The client

Throughout my years of organizing people, I've learned that there are certain factors that determine whether an organizing project will be easy or hard, go quickly or take a tediously long time, bring forth a lot of awareness or increase the resistance, and increase or decrease cooperation.

One of the factors that determine whether a project will be easy and fast, or difficult and slow is if the person chose to get organized on their own or the choice was made for them by someone else. In my experience, the clients that were forced or emotionally manipulated by someone else to get organized almost always turned out to be the most difficult projects that took longer than necessary. They also seem to be the people that were most numb to their environments and the least aware of how they have been contributing to the problem and its impact on themselves and the people in their lives.

Such is the case for Sue. Sue had been married to Jim for over 20 years and had two teenagers living at home. She was retired from the military, and was now a full-time housewife who spent her days feeding her out of control shopping addiction and cleaning her home OCD style (ya know, the type of detail where toothpicks are involved). Jim, her husband, spent his days still serving in the military where he worked to support her spending habit, and he had become weary of the hoarding he was forced to endure day after day, month after month, year after year. A seemingly agreeable man, Jim finally reached his breaking point and decided to take back the control in his home by setting an ultimatum that unless Sue agreed to allow a Professional Organizer to deal with her clutter and hoarding he would divorce her. Reluctantly she agreed, I was called in and that's when one of my most challenging projects began.

The assessment

Pulling up to their large and attractive home with it's perfectly manicured landscaping and located in a wealthier area of San Diego, I was about to see how deceiving outward appearances can be.

As many of my clients do, when Sue greeted me, she flung open the door and started nervously talking a mile a minute as if she was trying to distract me from seeing the condition of her home. But she could have had an elephant standing in her living room and it still wouldn't have blocked me from seeing the calamity she had built up around her.

Every corner, countertop, table, shelf, floor space, wall space, back space, side space, cabinet, and closet was full of stuff, stuff, and more stuff. Finding even a few inches of clear space was like trying to find the Holy Grail. The feeling of overwhelm was so unmistakable that even I, with all the experience I have being in many disorganized and cluttered environments, stood in bewilderment that someone could live with so much stuff.

Her kitchen was stocked with enough cleaning supplies, baking ingredients, storage containers, cooking utensils, and appliances that it could have easily supplied four households for many years.

On top of the kitchen, with a well stocked pantry of cleaning supplies, a living room with a ten foot long china cabinet full of *tchotckes* (or, as some people call them knickknacks), an office where an entire five-drawer file cabinet was jammed with greeting cards and boxes of paperwork everywhere, the garage, however, is what earned her the gold medal of hoarding award.

It wasn't even how much stuff she had that blew my mind. It was the quantity of particular items she had that made me realize I was dealing with someone who had a pretty severe hoarding problem. As an example, not only did she have a 66-quart storage container full of backpacks, she had ten of them. TEN! The garage even came complete with an inoperable VW bug that was used to hold even more stuff, which made moving around the garage very difficult.

News flash! Garages were meant for cars.

Here's an interesting fact. A survey done by the U.S. Department of Energy reports that 25% of people, with two-car garages don't park in it and that 32% parked only one car in their garage.

I think this quote by former President of The National Association of Professional Organizers pretty much sums up what American garages have become.

The irony is that people are leaving their expensive cars in the driveway or on the street, yet their garages are full of worthless junk.

Now, I know none of us like to think of the stuff in our garages as junk, but I think most of you would agree that at least 25% will never be used again and therefore it's more junk than not junk.

After my initial assessment, I determined that this project was going to take at least three Organizers working six hours a day for almost two weeks to finish, and that's if we were really focused, and got Sue's total cooperation. Although my optimistic side wanted to believe otherwise, my gut told me that she was going to fight till the death to hold on to her stuff, and, boy, was I right. One of the few times in my life that I didn't relish being right.

Does it make you feel good or bad?

I can confidently say that I have a pretty good track record of helping people to see the wisdom in letting go of the stuff that no longer serves them. The approach I use comes mainly from an energetic perspective. Of course, I will use the traditional line of questioning like how long have you had this, will you use it again, and what will you use it for? But what I have found to be far more effective is getting people to understand the energy they direct towards their belongings and the negative affect it may be creating in their space and lives.

When I started to notice the connection between the condition of someone's space and the things in that space had a lot to do with how they felt about it, I started to do some research on this fascinating concept. What I have found is emotions carry a vibration that will energetically imprint on to the spaces you are in and can change the vibration of the space in either a positive or negative way depending on whether it is a low vibration emotion or a high one. In other words, the emotions you feel towards your things are leaving their mark in your home which may be causing your home to feel good or bad. This is often referred to as energetic imprinting.

Depression, anger, and fear are examples of low vibration emotions. High vibration emotions would feel like happiness, joy, and love. Based on this concept, when a client seems like they are having a tough time deciding whether to keep an item or not I simply ask if it makes them feel good or bad. The answer that follows often reveals the source of the low vibration emotion that the person has not consciously been paying attention to.

It might sound like this, "I loved this dress when I bought it and it cost a lot of money, but I haven't worn it in a while because it makes me feel old when I do." In this example, feeling old while wearing the dress is the low vibration emotion. Feeling like money is being wasted by getting rid of the dress would also be another low vibration emotion. Instead of listening to the reasons why the dress doesn't work for them, they tend to listen to the reasons why they "shouldn't" get rid of it in an effort to postpone having to make the uncomfortable, and maybe painful, decision to let it go.

They may have postponed the decision to let the thing go, but because the emotion got imprinted, it will continue to affect the space, causing the person to feel bad. Feeling bad often makes it difficult to find the energy and focus to clean and organize a home.

Even when someone is trying to hide their emotions, I can usually tell which things are causing a person to feel good or bad based on their body language, tone of voice, and energy when they talk about it. If they are willing to listen, I will bring the observation to their awareness and help shed some light on why they can't seem to let something go.

From there, I encourage them to have an out loud conversation with themselves so they can hear the truth being revealed as they give the reasons why they are holding on to something. Then I help them to see the connection between their emotions and the negative affect it may be creating in their life and how it's showing up in their space.

At that point, it could go one of three ways. Some people will decide the possession is not worth the energetic block and choose to let it go immediately. Others will decide that they can't get rid of it, but are at least willing to remove it from their valuable real estate areas and make a decision on it again in three months. Finally, there will be the person that will dig in their heels, and not only insist the item stays, but stay right where it is.

Before I begin the organizing process, I will do what I call the walk and talk with the client. This is where I take a notepad and together we walk around their home as I let them say whatever they think and feel about the spaces and stuff in their home. Inevitably, they will almost always use the word hate during the process. At the end of the walk and talk, I present them with how many times they said they hated or expressed negative feelings towards their spaces and stuff. The client is often surprised at the amount of negative emotion they are experiencing in their homes and begin to finally understand why they may be experiencing difficulties in their life.

Exercise: The "I Hate" list

To bring to your awareness how many negative emotions you are feeling in your home, take a notepad and walk around each room. Every time you hear yourself thinking or feeling a negative emotion like hate write it down. You may hear yourself saying things like:

- "I hate that picture but my husband won't take it down because his mom gave it to him."
- "That chair is so old, ugly and uncomfortable I never feel like sitting in it."
- "I hate going into that room because it's so dark and depressing."
- "Someday I might get back into these jeans but I have no time to work out and I keep getting fatter and fatter."
- "I hate that every time I try to file papers into the filing cabinet the drawer falls off the track."
- "I should finish this baby book but I don't even like scrapbooking anymore."
- "I know Jake's baby clothes are taking up a lot of space but I'll feel guilty if I get rid of them."

To completely receive the full benefits of doing this exercise, you will need to wear your honest Abe hat and walk around your spaces without judgment but rather a commitment to uncovering the truth. Express your thoughts and feelings out loud and really listen to what you are saying. You may be surprised what you hear. Even if you don't make the changes right away to change a space or remove the things that are making you feel bad, awareness is everything and that's a good place to start.

The standoff

Sue wasn't interested in hearing her self-talk to uncover her negative emotions. She seemed only interested in doing the bare minimum she felt necessary in order to appease her husband's demands.

Within two hours of sorting through the items in the living room, I realized she wasn't budging a bit. I usually start to see progress from the client within 30 minutes to one hour of starting, but not with Sue. Nothing was getting purged.

At that point, I turned to her and said, "Sue, you aren't getting rid of anything are you?" With a smug look on her face she said, "Nope." With that, I said, "Okay, I can still get your place organized, but it's going to make it a lot harder." She simply stated, "Well, my husband is the one who wanted this not me." She had just admitted that resentment was a big factor in her resistance to my assistance.

The sabotage with stuff strategy

I've only had a few clients that were really stubborn and would hardly let anything go. Interestingly enough, these clients were the ones who expressed a lot of resentment and blamed the condition of their home on everyone and everything else. They also seemed to have a high need to control everything and everyone around them and would often act emotionally unstable.

It was still too early to know whether or not I could help her, but I was determined to conquer that house and open her eyes to her clutter and hoarding problem. Thankfully, she put her resistance down long enough to explain to me that for a long time she had wanted to move from that house, but her husband wouldn't do it. I could now see where the resentment was coming from and it explained why the condition of her home was showing signs of sabotage, using stuff to punish and seek revenge. Recognizing that our clutter is our mostly unconscious emotions expressed, I can almost guarantee the unconscious belief she had going round and round in her brain was saying, "Okay, Jim, if you don't want to move into a home that I want, then why should I give you the clean and organized home that you want?" So, consciously or not, she made her house uncomfortable for him to live in as a way of expressing her resentment.

This resentment against her husband, however, was clearly not her only emotional blockage. Looking at her massive amounts of stuff, some of it so precisely organized in her own way, I saw that there was also hoarding issues in play.

Poverty and hoarding

The type of hoarding behavior Sue displayed is common for people who grew up poor, which she revealed she had. I've organized many people who grew up poor and became hoarders later in life. They are so terrified of being without, that letting something go of something they might need is perceived as a threat to their very survival. This survival and scarcity mentality will affect every area of their life including money, relationships, career, and health, and cause them to hoard things as a way to avoid feeling lack in their life.

Times of scarcity are not new, but living in scarcity today does not look the same as the scarcity our previous generations experienced. The difference is now we have the ability to buy anything we want by just clicking a button. Combine consumerism with mental programming that tells someone they are bad in some way for letting something go, or not having enough and *voila,* you have the recipe for a potential hoarder.

Growing up in poverty contributed to Sue's tendencies to also hoard food. Her childhood home was far from town, making stocking up on groceries a once a month event. As a result, there were times when the food supply was low, and the family was forced to be as resourceful as possible with their food consumption. In an effort to avoid feeling the pain of having an empty pantry, she continued the pattern of stocking up on food in large amounts, even though she had a store right down the street. Sue's experience in childhood created a fear of not having enough food to eat, and as a result, she went to the extremes and overstocked. Ironically, this was the one spot in the house she kept meticulously organized.

I've found that even though the majority of someone's home might be disorganized, there may be certain spots that are kept

Chapter 3

very neat and organized. Interestingly enough, I've noticed those same areas are the ones people seem to like the most. Like the husband who won't pick up after himself, but keeps his tool area in the garage totally organized, or the teenager with a messy room but makes sure his car is always showroom floor ready.

Poverty doesn't only apply to physical things. Emotional impoverishment can have an impact on organization later on in life too. I find many problems with clutter could be traced back to childhood issues that were never resolved. If a person experienced emotional deprivation in their childhood, then how they see the world will be colored with lack. For someone with hoarding tendencies, that will translate into a life controlled by stuff.

It is a necessary part of the organizing process to let people get out what they need to get out emotionally, and I encourage it. I once had a client with whom I would spend two of the four hours of our scheduled session sitting on the couch, letting her cry, and listening to the heartbreak she felt over her husband who died three years previously, and her current love interest who she was having difficulties with. In fact, I've shed many tears with my clients, but at the end of the day, my goal is to help move them into action so we can work on de-cluttering and organizing their homes. Sometimes, though, people are so emotionally stuck or resistant that they are incapable of making the number of decisions required to get through the process.

Though, I am a Professional Organizer with a hero complex, and I like to think I know a thing or two about helping people with their emotions, I also know when it's time to take off the cape and suggest to the client they seek counseling or other professional intervention. I'll explain to them that they will have better success at getting and staying organized after they have spent some time working on their internal issues. When they feel more emotionally secure and ready, they will see better results with their project.

I wasn't sure yet, whether Sue would require this recommendation.

Progress not perfection

Much to my surprise, Sue eventually got rid of a very small amount of stuff. I could have done a cartwheel when she finally decided to let something go, but in order to have organized her home in the most efficient, esthetically pleasing and functional way possible, she really needed to get rid of a lot more.

Sue was so strong willed when pleading her case to keep her stuff and justifying her purchases that, after a while, it became useless to even try to change her mind. Even when we organized her mounds of greeting cards, and I suggested that she had more than enough to last for a while, she still went out and bought more. I couldn't help but feel doing so was an act of defiance towards her husband, the process, and me! As much as I tried, I found it challenging to not take it personally.

I know that sometimes during the process clients might not like me very much because I'm pushing them out of their comfort zones and pushing their emotional hot buttons. They may even direct their negative feelings towards me. I once was talking to a woman with my arms crossed in her garage because I was cold. With an agitated tone, she said to me, "Look at you standing there with that Professional Organizer stance." I said, "Judy, it's because I'm cold, that's it." I know dealing with someone's misdirected negative emotions comes with being a Professional Organizer. Getting organized can be a very emotional process, so dealing with misdirected emotions is just part of the job.

Through the creative efforts of the organizing team I had helping me, we were able to find ways to put a lot of stuff into small and limited spaces, yet still organizing it so that she could access and put it all away easier than before. It wasn't the dramatic WOW effect I go for when I organize a space, but enough clear spaces were created that it was apparent we had made progress.

Though we did the best we could to set up Sue's home so it would be easier and faster for her to maintain, I knew it was only a matter of time before it would return to the same condition. Without addressing the resentment she was feeling over her husband's unwillingness to buy another home and other clutter causing beliefs buried deep below the surface, she would more than likely act out again by sabotaging the home with clutter. And it would probably happen instantly.

In the garage, when it was all said and done, I had to persuade her to rent another storage unit just to store all of her Christmas ornaments and gifts she had bought but couldn't give away in an attempt to create space for the stuff she wanted to keep closest to her.

I found Sue's behavior through the process fascinating. One of her behaviors, I jokingly refer to as the "chipmunk grab and stash" was where I would hold something up and ask her what it was and she would rush over, grab it from my hand and say, "Oh that goes in blankety blank" and then off she ran, to put God knows what into God knows where.

Another behavior I observed was what appeared to me to be the psychological condition obsessive compulsive disorder, or OCD. I have never seen a place so overwhelmed with stuff, yet so clean at the same time. The only dirt I found was the space between the fridge and the kitchen counter. Although her home was riddled with clutter, oddly enough, she was obsessive about keeping things clean.

When I found a bag of coins, she HAD to wash them on the spot. Probably the most unusual thing I found was she had taken the clips from plastic bread bags, cleaned them, and put them away in plastic storage bags.

When she stored items away, she would put baby diapers in with the box to absorb the moisture. Not a bad idea right? But when I saw she was also using diapers to absorb the moisture in teapots, I had to question whether this was OCD, or just a really clever trick I never learned. I'm not a professional teapot maker so I could be wrong, but I would bet that moisture damage is not a common problem with teapots.

With three Organizers, working 12-days, for 6.5 hours a day, we had managed to organize the majority of Sue's home and garage.

Within that time frame, we still had not even touched the boxes and boxes of paperwork we had collected.

Her husband was ecstatic with the results and our efforts seemed to have saved the marriage for now, but I knew that if she continued to satisfy her addiction of buying and collecting things, and most likely she would, her house would become cluttered again.

Although she expressed some gratitude for the work we had done, I don't think she truly understood the value of it. Had she been the one to make the decision to say she was ready to get organized I know that it would have been a different story. Readiness, willingness, and desire are everything when it comes to getting organized.

I have checked in with her several times since, and she is still convinced she can handle the rest on her own. I think we both know she really doesn't have the capacity or willingness to get organized on her own, but I also know being honest with herself about that was probably not going to happen. I'll admit, it bothers me when clients don't see how much they are in need of help, but I can't force someone to accept my, or anyone else's help and that is challenging for me to deal with at times.

As a Professional Organizer it is always my goal to not only get my clients organized, but set them up to keep them organized. I work to transform their physical environments into spaces that will be a lot easier to maintain, reduce their stress, help them feel more comfortable, and enjoy their lives more. But staying organized requires not only working on the outside but working on the inside too. Unfortunately, if the client isn't willing to do the internal work to change their behaviors and mindset, I know that sustainable results will be less likely.

Realistically, the habits, behaviors, and mindset responsible for creating their clutter will not change overnight. However, it's about progress not perfection. Even if they only experienced minor changes and mini-breakthroughs, it's a step in the right direction towards overcoming their organizing obstacles. Those steps may lead them down a path that helps to save their marriage, family, career, health, happiness, and, maybe, even their life.

Diapers, Toothpicks, and Bread Clips, Oh My! TAKE AWAYS

1. A survey done by the U.S. Department of Energy reports that 25% of people, with two-car garages don't park in it and that 32% parked only one car in their garage.

2. Emotions carry either a low or high vibration. These vibrations will imprint themselves into our spaces and things and will create a negative or positive affect in our lives depending on whether the emotion is a low or high vibration. This is called energetic imprinting.

3. When you are having a tough time making a decision whether you should keep something or not, ask yourself if it makes you feel good or bad. Listen to yourself talk out loud when you are explaining the reasons why so you can really hear the subconscious beliefs driving your decisions.

4. To avoid feeling the pain of letting something go, people often choose to listen to their reasons for holding on, rather than listening to the truth of how it really makes them feel.

5. Driven by resentment and anger, a person may unconsciously use what I call the "sabotage with stuff strategy" as an act of rebellion and defiance.

6. Although the whole house may be disorganized, there may be certain areas that are kept neat and organized. Those are the areas people typically express very positive feelings towards.

7. Those who have grown up poor often develop hoarding and cluttering tendencies out of fear of being without and can perceive letting something go as a threat to their survival.

8. A good majority of cluttering tendencies have connections to childhood issues that never got resolved, and reflect a mentality of emotional deprivation.

9. Readiness, willingness, and desire are everything when it comes to getting organized.

10. Sometimes, a Professional Organizer is not enough. Counseling or therapy may be necessary to bring someone to the state of readiness to tackle their stuff and the emotional issues underlying the clutter and hoarding.

11. Getting organized is not an overnight process. Along with external changes, it also requires an internal change of habits, behaviors and mindset. Making even minor changes is a step in the right direction towards overcoming organizing obstacles.

~ ~ ~ ~ ~ ~ ~ ~

"If you find a menorah anywhere put it aside cuz I need to have one out for when my mom gets here."

Client Quote

"I have a bag for my bags and I have a fetish for scissors & flashlights."

Client Quote

"You can judge the state of a woman's mind by the state of her closet."

Coco Chanel

A Part of Me

Chapter 4

The client

Debbie was a very petite, soft spoken, married woman in her 50's who was a massage therapist. She and I met when I did a speaking engagement on organizing at a local college. She called me the next day because a lot of what I said really hit home with her.

Our conversation lasted an hour and we uncovered a lot. She revealed to me that her husband was very frustrated with her and her clutter, even leaving at one point because of it, but he had never done anything to help her with it. My gut told me that her husband was mirroring the relationship she had with her parents and this was driving some of her clutter behavior. This was confirmed when she shared that she felt that, like her mother, she had a husband who was a rager who constantly put her down, further injuring what seemed to be her already fragile self-esteem. This low self–esteem, I suspected, is what drove her need to fill the void with stuff.

The revelations about her husband left me concerned about how successful the project would be for her. If her husband did not support her efforts, or if he continued to degrade her, I feared she would continue to fill the emotional void with clutter and all our hard work would be buried under more clutter.

The June Cleaver standard

If a partner does not support an organizing project it can have a very big impact on the progress and sustaining any results. That is why one of the first questions I always ask someone during the initial assessment is if the prospective client's partner or other household members know they are calling me, and, if so, how do they feel about bringing in a Professional Organizer.

I began that practice after a particular client experience. Once, when I was on a project the wife casually told me, "Oh, by the way, my husband is coming home shortly and he has no idea that I have hired you." Gulp! Talk about a surprise. That made me very uncomfortable because I had no idea if her husband would come home and be upset that I was there, and what the consequences might be. To both of our delights, and shock, he was totally on board and wound up throwing half of his garage away. Not only that, but I was able to get her normally disinterested teenage sons to help, too. It was a kumbaya moment for sure, but after that, I vowed to not let myself get ambushed like that again.

Many times, I have found the husbands are resistant to the idea of hiring a Professional Organizer to help their wives get the house organized. Often, there is an expectation that maintaining a clean and organized home "should" be easy for the wife to handle on her own simply because she's a woman. It's as if society still places a standard on women that they should run their home like June Cleaver from the *Leave it to Beaver* show. Making sure by the time their husband comes home, the house and children are clean, dinner is cooked, and she's waiting at the door with his scotch and slippers, ready to meet his every need.

Never mind the fact that today, many women are also holding down full time jobs and running businesses, while still caring for their families, and maintaining a household. It causes a lot of tension in the house, and in the marriage, and could cause self esteem issues in women because they too think they "should" be able to perform a role that is traditionally the woman's responsibility.

Additionally, consideration is not being given to the fact that maybe she was never taught how to clean and organize. Maybe she grew up in a disorganized and cluttered household where she watched one or both of her parents model disorganized behavior.

If someone grows up with an alcoholic parent, the chances of that person growing up and also becoming an alcoholic, or getting into a relationship with an alcoholic increases. It's no different for someone growing up with someone who hoards, clutters, and is disorganized.

The next time you find yourself getting ready to whip out the baseball bat for another self esteem beat down for not keeping your home organized and clean like a "real woman" should, take a breath, and take a moment to remind yourself that it's old programming and behaviors and, no matter what, you can change them.

The more people who do the work to break old family patterns of cluttering, hoarding and disorganization, the better chance we have of saving our future generations from getting buried by stuff.

The assessment

Our initial session was only a targeted consultation, and just like in the phone conversation a lot was revealed.

Debbie had told me over the phone that she had a particular affinity for buying clothes and had requested that I come and help her organize her closet. When I visited her, I learned just how much of an affinity with clothes she had.

As she flipped on the light in her walk in closet, it was apparent that her need to feed her self esteem had a strong hold on her. The closet was about 6x5x10 in size, with a dark and heavy feeling created by the wood paneling. Her shrine to clothes consisted of several rows of hanging clothes, all jam-packed together, plastic drawers on the ground with, yep, you got it, more clothes, lots of shoes, and purses galore. All of this didn't even account for the additional clothes that were sitting outside of the closet in chest of drawers, plastic bins, and even on the pool table. Even though she had quite a bit of clothes, I've seen more extreme cases of clothes hoarding.

That title would go to a woman whose closet was so gigantic that it was the size of a small bedroom. I'm not kidding. That wasn't even enough space for her. She had clothes hanging on garment racks inside the closet as well and more accessories then I've even seen a store have on display. I'd love to be a fly on the wall on one of her shopping sprees. I can just see the foam coming out of the sides of her mouth as she gets ready to kill that zebra patterned purse.

Oh, the savagery of shopping.

The action

Debbie's closet was organized, but she just had too much stuff and needed help letting go. Rather than digging in and starting the purging, we spent the first two hours doing what was more like closet therapy.

She proceeded to tell me how she had been very poor growing up and couldn't afford to shop in the same stores that a lot of her classmates were shopping at, and that made her feel embarrassed. To add to that, she was very insecure about her looks. Her father would constantly tease her, even calling her names like ugly duckling.

Very self aware, Debbie shared with me a life altering memory of her dad making a comment about a dress she had been wearing and how pretty she looked in it. It was in that moment she made the connection that how pretty she looked was based on what she was wearing. This belief played a major role in creating her clothes hoarding tendencies and low self-esteem.

Debbie also struggled with identity issues. She seemed overly concerned about what people, especially her husband, thought about the way she looked. Consequently, she felt anxiety about wearing some of the clothes she really liked. As she looked at different pieces of clothing, she would continually say things like, "A part of me really likes this but it's too sexy" or "I use to ballroom dance and a part of me really wants to dance again, but my husband won't come dancing with me."

She also explained she had a frequent habit of impulsively buying clothes that appealed to parts of her personality she would often hide. Once she tried them on at home, her fears around what others would think would surface and into the closet they went along with all the other "I like it but" clothes. More on that later.

After a couple hours getting to the root of her clothes hoarding problem, she agreed to pick a small area and purge whatever she felt she could. She was able to get rid of a few things pretty easily. This made me think that future purging sessions would be a breeze. You won't hear me say this often, but I was wrong.

Lack of confidence clutter

What I realized is Debbie had many different aspects of her personality that wanted to be expressed and accepted. However, receiving the message in childhood that it wasn't okay for her to be herself, she unconsciously shut parts of herself down and hid them. She didn't have the confidence to express them when and how she felt like it.

I speculated that her insatiable drive to hoard clothes may have been driven by an unconscious need to earn her father's love and attention by wearing something pretty.

Women's closets are an interesting place to me. I love working in them because I feel the condition of this space mirrors how they feel about themselves and how they consciously or unconsciously choose to show up in the world. Does she have clothes that need mending, clothes that don't fit, uncomfortable shoes, jewelry that is just thrown in a box, outdated clothes, items that she doesn't really like, clothes that don't feel good or look good, hand me downs that she's keeping out of guilt, no accessories, wire hangers, no colorful clothing, very little clothing, or, as in Debbie's case, way too much clothing? It all makes a statement about her and how she goes about her life.

Although she was aware that shopping for clothes had become out of control, she had found herself unable to stop. By getting clear in her closet, so to speak, she was really starting to see how much power she was giving to the opinion of others about the way she looked. This gave her a lot to digest during the months between our sessions.

Back to the action

By the time she had me over again, she had done a complete remodel of her master bathroom and closet. Although narrow, the closet gained more space by adding shelves, an upper storage area, and extending the hanging space. It also now had a window that really brightened it up. She had done a major purge and gotten rid of at least ten bags of clothing, but the closet was still jam-packed full of clothes, and she needed to purge more.

During the remodel, the closet had become somewhat disorganized again. As we continued doing more closet therapy, I organized her clothes into like categories.

Closet organizing tip

In closets, the standard order that clothes are hung is short to long, light to dark and of course all like items together, for example, all short sleeves together, long sleeves, shorts, and so on. Sometimes, if space is an issue, I will store seasonal items in a plastic container and place them either up high in their bedroom closet or in some other area of the home to free up space in the valuable real estate areas.

Valuable real estate, in organizing lingo, refers to the areas that you can access easily. In these areas, it's best to store items you access frequently and not items you don't access frequently. For example, tying up your bedroom closet shelves with Christmas ornaments isn't an efficient use of that space, whereas putting extra blankets you would use in that bedroom would be.

Interestingly enough, on one of my speaking engagements I used that example and a husband quickly turned to his wife and said, "We need to hire her." Why? Because they had Christmas ornaments on the shelves in their bedroom cabinets.

Office supplies are another example of this. Have an office supply zone where you can put your overflow offices supplies rather than having all five boxes of staples sitting in your desk drawer frees up a lot of valuable space. This way you have room for items that you will need to access more frequently, like a stapler and calculator.

The "big but strategy"

As we were in her closet, I made several attempts to see if she was ready to let clothing go. I treaded lightly and decided not to push too hard for fear that it might bruise her already fragile self esteem. After about two hours of gently questioning her whether she was ready, still no progress had been made. She then became frustrated because she felt the organizing I did in her closet was something she could have done on her own and that her money was being wasted. She was hoping for some big breakthrough to happen and she expected that I was the one who was supposed to make that happen.

I admit, I got frustrated over the fact that I'd been gently pushing her to let stuff go, but she wasn't responding and now it felt like she was blaming me at the lack of progress as though I was responsible for her decisions. As a result, I decided to turn it up a notch. I felt nervous in doing this because I was afraid it may be more then she could handle. I'm pretty good at gauging the level of intensity I can use on my clients, but I had underestimated Debbie's tolerance levels.

It turned out being tougher was exactly what she needed. She needed me to be more assertive and brutally honest. With that, I challenged her on every piece of clothing she had in her closet. When she picked it up and said, "I like this, but" I would get her to elaborate more on the "but." Pretty soon we used the "but" as a way to decide whether a piece of clothing was a keeper or a tosser.

This is where I first took notice of when people sometimes use the word "but" when talking about their stuff. As a result, I now use what I call the "big but strategy" to help bring awareness to the negative emotions a person may be feeling towards their stuff and space when we are going through the purging phase.

Exercise 1: Find your "big buts"

Go through each item in your closet and ask yourself, "Do I love it and use it?" If you hear yourself say, "but" or "should" in your answer to explain why you are holding on to it, consider letting it go. If letting it go is too difficult for you, at least consider taking it out of your valuable real estate area and storing in a non-valuable real estate area like the top shelf of your closet or garage. Having a closet of only items you love and use will make a big difference in how you look and feel every day. Guaranteed!

Buying questions

We then decided that anything she could easily say she loved or at least really liked and wore at least once a year was a keeper. After that we established new criteria for when she wanted to purchase an article of clothing. She agreed to no longer buy something simply because she liked it, or because it was on sale. Now, instead of making an impulsive purchase, she agreed to ask herself a series of questions before buying anything. Questions like:

- How does it make me feel when I wear it?
- Does it fit me right?
- Does it feel comfortable wearing it?
- Do I have room for it where I can find and put it away easily?
- Do I already have something similar to it?
- Am I buying this because I like it or because I think someone else would like it for me?
- Can I afford it?

Exercise 2: Questions on the go

Print out and carry with you in your purse or wallet or add to your phone the list of questions from above to take with you while shopping. Having these questions with you will help you make smarter buying decisions based on reason instead of making an impulse buy based on emotion.

Progress is progress

Though getting organized often brings incredible transformation and awareness to one's life and sometimes instantly, there are no guarantees it will. The more open and willing someone is to change, the greater the potential for massive transformation and a new awareness to occur.

By working with Debbie, I realized that some clients are going to be looking for massive transformation by using a quick fix approach. I've learned that setting realistic expectations and constantly reminding them of the progress is necessary when working with people who tend to be the type who want everything to be fixed and done right away. Even if progress is small, progress is progress. Small steps of progress can have just as much of a positive impact on one's life as a massive breakthrough does.

As I mentioned before, I always have a take away when I work with a client that helps me to grow personally and professionally. I realized that even though someone is battling with low self-esteem, it doesn't mean they are not capable of handling a dose of tough love. For some people, that is the only way they will have breakthroughs and experience changes. I continue to work on mastering the art of delivering effective tough love and I'm very grateful for the lesson I learned through working with Debbie.

The results

Debbie wound up getting rid of two hundred and fifty pieces of clothing. That's two hundred and fifty above and beyond the ten bags she had already gotten rid of before my return visit. I knew this because she decided to itemize them for a tax deduction and it turned out to be a significant amount of money she was able to apply towards the tax deduction.

When it was all said and done, she was quite pleased with how many clothes she was able to let go of. On top of that, she also felt confident that she would give more thought to her future purchases rather than buying impulsively based on an emotional decision. Most importantly, she started to value herself more, not for what she wears but for who she is. Each and every part of her.

A Part of Me TAKE AWAYS

1. The support of a partner can have a big impact on the progress of an organizing project. A lack of support will make progress and sustaining the results harder.

2. There is a still an attitude that remains in our culture today that women should be able to keep a clean and organized home, regardless of how many more responsibilities women have in today's day and age. I call that the 'June Cleaver standard'. Additionally, she may have never been taught how to clean and organize a home because she grew up with parents who modeled disorganized and clutter behavior.

3. A single experience in our lives can cause us to form certain beliefs about ourselves and others, which then go on to shape our behaviors and attitudes.

4. Low self-esteem can cause someone to hide certain parts of who they really are and make their decisions based on what other people think about them.

5. There seems to be a connection between the condition of a woman's closet and how she feels about herself. It also reflects how she consciously or unconsciously chooses to show up in the world.
6. In closets, the standard order that clothes are hung is short

to long, light to dark and combining items that are similar together. For example all short sleeves together, long sleeves, shorts, and so on.

7. An area that you can access easily is called, in organizing lingo, valuable real estate. This is an area where only items that need to be accessed frequently should go.

8. Using the "big but strategy" will help you to identify which items you are having negative emotions towards. If there is a "but" in your reasoning about keeping or getting rid of an item, identify if the but is valid, positive, or negative, and act accordingly.

9. To prevent impulse spending, it's best to ask questions that are based on logic instead of pure emotion. Print out the "Buying Questions" listed earlier in this chapter, and keep them in your purse, wallet, or phone to reference when you are making a decision on buying something.

10. Although massive breakthroughs and changes are pretty common when de-cluttering and organizing, you may need to use tough love on yourself in order to get them. This is where working with a Professional Organizer can really help.

"So what's the prognosis? How long do we have to live before we drown?"

Client Quote

"You should change your name to Miss Indispensable."

Client Quote

"Where should I put my wine glasses? ... oh I know next to my meds."

Client Quote

"You are going to be the one to tell my husband because he'll listen to you. He thinks you walk on water."

Client Quote

"Your purse is a portable microcosm of your either feeling organized and light on your feet or weighed down and chaotic."

Julie Morgenstern

"Your house is your home only when you feel you have jurisdiction over the space."

Joan Kron

Stranger Danger

Chapter 5

The client

A divorced mother of two boys and in her late forties, Leslie felt that she received a message from the Universe that it was time for her to reach out for help and hire a Professional Organizer.

Like most of my clients, she kept plodding along believing that she should be able to get organized on her own. Independent, smart, and headstrong, it had long made no sense to her why she couldn't just get it done. A former Wall Street employee and business owner, she longed to live the organized and minimalist life she once had. But she also realized after battling Lyme disease for many years, that although she once could tackle any project with gusto she just didn't have it in her anymore to tackle hardly anything beyond mere survival.

Leslie's decision to finally take action was motivated by the lease on her rental home coming to an end and a desire to start off in her new place with a clean slate. In order to do that, before she called me she already knew she would need to get rid of the items that she felt a negative attachment towards. Those items were primarily located in her garage, which was filled with furniture from her very difficult marriage that she was in the process of ending. She felt depressed and stressed, and it was taking an even greater toll on her health, and her relationship with her children. That's when I got the call that she needed to get rid of the items in her garage and help with the moving process.

Leslie and I developed a deep connection over the phone almost immediately, and she told me that she knew the Universe would bring the right person to help her. After talking briefly she conveyed to me that she knew, without a doubt, that I was the right person.

The story she proceeded to share with me absolutely blew my mind and showed me the strength and perseverance she had. Leslie told me that after battling Lyme disease for years, that not only did it get passed on to her kids *in utero*, it also caused a lot of damage to her immune system and affected her brain causing ADHD like symptoms.

The onset of the disease was very sudden. One day, she was sitting by herself at home when she started to feel very ill. She walked over to the couch and before her head could hit the pillow she felt like a lightning bolt had gone through her head. Leslie thought she was having a stroke.

She told me that she called her husband at work to tell him something was wrong, to which he coldly responded by telling her to call 911. After she asked him to call for her because she couldn't get her fingers to work, she wound up falling to the floor where paralysis started to set in and move its way up from her toes to her neck. In that moment she would have her first experience with what she believed was her angel speaking and heard a voice tell her "Do not be afraid." The paramedics finally showed up and by this time she was unable to move or even speak. Her husband never came home from work.

Fast forward a couple of years later, after a period of intense stress, the paralysis returned. While on bed rest for weeks, she received very minimal care and developed bed sores as a result of spending days in her own bodily fluids. When she came down with pneumonia and ran a 104-degree temperature, it was her son that had to tell his dad "Mommy is too hot." Again, her husband acted indifferent, and had to be told to call 911 by his son after asking, "Well, what do you want me to do about it?" After a couple of hours, she woke up in the ER to find herself in an ice bath and her husband sitting next to her working on his laptop. She said, "I had a weird dream that you are going to divorce me." His reply? "Yes, I am."

After a couple of months of bed rest and recovering from her bed sores, she had her second experience with her angel. This time it said, "It's time to stand up." She said, "I can't." It said, "You don't have to." From there she was able to get up on her own two feet and that's where her healing journey began.

It's hard to believe at the time we met, that only one year previously she was in a wheelchair. Now, although her pace was slow, she was full of determination to conquer the clutter she knew was affecting her negatively on all levels.

The assessment

Many times, the garages I've been in are dirty with really old stuff, shoved together and completely neglected. The majority of them aren't used for the purpose they are intended for - actually storing a car. Leslie's garage however, had very nice things like some of her expensive furniture that was still sitting in the garage from her move one year prior. She also had leftover items from her previous home decorating business sitting on metal shelves.

Within a few moments of stepping into her garage, we started talking about why she was holding on to some of these items. She specifically pointed to several containers holding fabric that were to be used for a crafting project. Leslie was able to immediately tap into her sense of failure of not having completed this one, of many, projects she had started.

Leslie then picked up a cane she had to use while she was sick, and although she didn't need to use it anymore, she voiced her concerns over letting it go by stating out loud what was going through her mind, "But what if I get sick again and might need it?" The whole I might need it someday is the number one phrase I hear when someone is afraid to let an item go.

I then asked "Well, what is the worst thing that would happen if you let it go?" She told me that she felt that on some level she would be ridiculed. That people would look at her and say, "Who do you think you are thinking you are getting better?"

What Leslie's comments conveyed to me was she was having a difficult time allowing herself to be okay with getting healthier. She was so stuck in the idea that she would never be healthy that she wasn't even allowing herself to recognize that not only was she already healthier, but that it was possible for her to continue to get even healthier. In talking it out her eyes opened very quickly to the prison her own mind had created.

Based on experience and intuition, I knew that boiling just beneath the surface of all of this negative self talk were mother control issues. Sure enough, as she continued to express the thoughts that were attached to her stuff, the role her mother played in all of this started to reveal itself.

The issue of her growing up with a parent with martyr tendencies surfaced when she picked up a bottle of decorative hand soap and was frustrated with herself that she was having a difficult time letting it go even though it had been unused and sitting in her garage for quite a while.

"I can't just throw it away because that's wasteful and I can't recycle it which will hurt the earth," she proclaimed.

It was just as I suspected! She had the whole she's gotta save the world mantra going on in her head.

In fact, when I brought this to her attention she said, "Well, I did want to feed all the starving kids in Africa when I was a kid."

With that, I helped her to see that this value of being the saver, can sometimes disguise itself as being valiant and honorable, when in fact it actually may not only be the good old manipulative tactic used by martyrs to instill guilt, but it also sets the martyr up for being the one to get hurt in their effort to save and protect.

The definition of martyr is *somebody who suffers persecution and death for other people*. Basically, serving others comes with a cost to the one serving. The interesting thing about martyrs is many times they really don't know that they are being manipulative, they really feel like they are helping, which makes it even more difficult to stand up to them and get them to stop.

As long as they perceive they are coming from a place of help, which may be their way of trying to show their love, then, in their minds, they are not doing anything wrong. So if you try to tell them they are wrong, then there is usually a big guilt trip that is laid on the one confronting the martyr.

Investigating further, I learned that yes, in fact, Leslie's mom was definitely a martyr and laid huge guilt treatments on her. This caused her to feel bad over anything she did that she perceived as not being helpful or self serving.

If her mom wasn't around to lay guilt on her, she was so programmed to feel guilty that she unconsciously created situations in her life to keep her locked in the feelings of guilt. Her unfinished projects were a symptom of this.

Projects and stress

The interesting thing about clutter is that where I see clutter, I also typically see lots of unfinished projects. They tend to go hand and hand.

Projects like filing papers, fixing furniture, selling items, creating baby books, and making a quilt out of t-shirts will have been sitting around for months, even years, while the clutter continues to pile up.

If these projects aren't being actively worked on or at least moving forward in some way, they will continue to take up space in the brain and create a vicious cycle of stress and overwhelm. This can lead to a paralyzing effect where decision making becomes more difficult, procrastination occurs, and the mental and emotional energy needed to tackle clutter, and work on projects gets drained. This can have physical effects, as well, such as tiredness and foggy thinking.

Stress, the brain and decision making

Let's talk a moment about how the brain and body react to stress and how it affects decision making.

The area of the brain where decision making and control of emotions occurs is called the pre-frontal lobe also known as the rational brain. A stress reaction in the body will cause a release of chemicals such as adrenaline and cortisol from the adrenal glands and prepares the body for a fight or flight response. This response serves as a protective mechanism against perceived danger. When this happens, the activity in the pre-frontal lobe shuts off, almost as if short circuited. At this point, the limbic system also known as the reptilian brain, takes over causing difficulty in decision making and keeping the emotions in check. We all know what happens when our emotions run amuck. We can't think straight and making a decision becomes harder. In this state of mind, we either make poor decisions or completely avoid making one altogether.

Evaluating the cost of a project

When taking on a project, it's important to first evaluate the return on investment so you can make a more informed decision on whether it's worth the cost of your time, money and energy. Asking yourself some key questions before you begin will save you from working on a project where the return on investment is low and the cost is high. Here's a list of questions you can ask:

1. What is my goal and why am I doing this project?

2. What do I expect to get out of working on it?

3. Do I have the time to work on it?

4. When will I schedule the time to work on this project?

5. When do I want to start and when do I want it completed by?

6. What are my anticipated expenses and do I have the money to pay for them?

7. How long will it take?

8. What resources do I need?

If you can stop yourself long enough before you dive into another project to ask these critical, time and money saving questions, it just may prevent you from looking at one more project that you haven't finished, feeling guilty or shameful about it, and continuing to drain your energy. Instead you can apply that energy towards other projects in your life that would yeild a higher return on investment.

I challenge you today to find at least one project you have not worked on in at least a year and make the decision to let it go. You won't believe how incredibly freeing it will feel when you do.

Back to the action

Once Leslie became aware of why she was hanging on to things, she did what most of my clients do when they finally wakeup and become conscious to their clutter causing thoughts. She started chucking.

Looking at her stuff through a new set of eyes, she than began to purge items she had been indecisively looking at for a while. She shocked herself how easily she was able to let go of the very things that were keeping her prisoner before. Imagine that. All that awareness got brought to the surface because of a plastic container of hand soap. Being emotionally attached to stuff is one of the main reasons why clutter and disorganization happen.

Because her belongings were pretty valuable, and she had less than a month before she had to move out, I recommended she use a consignment store to help her sell her belongings instead of selling them individually on Craigslist, or doing a garage sale.

During this process, I had an opportunity to interact and watch the interaction between her and her two sons; Joseph, 10, and Cameron, 15. There was a moment of frustration she experienced when Joseph kept interrupting us as she was trying to make a decision, and as a result she snapped at him.

He was upset because some books of his had been given away. Leslie justified giving them away because he had never looked at them. In fact, it wasn't until her mom had come into town and made a big deal over the books, using her normal strategy of guilt, that he started making a big deal over the books, too. Again, proving how some adults can project their attachment to things on to kids and cause them to have attachments that may not have been there before. Rather than acknowledging his feelings, she barked at him and minimized them.

Imposing beliefs

Rather than him being upset that he no longer got to read the books, I couldn't help but wonder if believing his grandma would be the person upset over getting rid of them was the real reason why for his emotional outburst. This is common because children are very susceptible to the beliefs and opinions adults in their lives have about physical possessions. Those beliefs play a role in forming what will be either a healthy or unhealthy relationship to stuff.

Projects where kids are involved are the most rewarding part of my job. They are usually really excited and open to learn what I have to teach them about organizing. They get excited over doing even the smallest of tasks like helping me put together boxes or separating hangers. I once had a client's 2½ year old cry as her parents were attempting to put her to sleep, "I want to stay up and clean with Tracy!" It was so friggin' adorable, and I felt so proud that I was able to help a kid enjoy organizing.

I also have found most of them really like and welcome the letting go process. Before we start, I make an agreement with the parents that they will let their kids have complete say on their own things and get to decide what stays and what goes without the parents input. Once their kids were given the freedom of choice, they were quite surprised to learn what they liked and didn't like.

From a single mother who discovered her 10-year old didn't like half the clothes in his closet, to a teenager whose rebellious tendencies were exacerbated by her room still being decorated with furniture from when she was five, kids definitely have an opinion about their stuff and their spaces. They just aren't always going to be vocal with their feelings for fear of getting yelled at, not being heard, or nothing being done about it at all.

On top of teaching kids organizing skills and guiding them through the letting go process, I also really enjoy helping the parents become aware of the language and behaviors they are using that could be unintentionally teaching and creating cluttering and disorganized tendencies in their kids. I only wish I had one of those nanny cams so they can really see and hear themselves in action.

Case in point was a garage project involving a pre-teen girl and her dad. A few days earlier, her mom and I had taken the girls clothes out of the car and sorted them into bankers boxes so she could do the next step of purging. During the next session in the garage, her dad looked at a box of clothes she had already purged and the following conversation occurred:

"Chelsea, do you want this or not?"

"No, Dad, I don't like it anymore."

"Well, does it fit?"

"Yes, it fits, but I don't want it anymore."

"Chelsea, we spent a lot of money on this are you sure you don't want it?"

"Yes, Dad I really don't want it anymore!"

"Well, I think we should keep it because it fits you and we spent a lot of money on it and you should be happy that you even have clothes to wear when other kids don't."

Later, when I approached him to bring some awareness to his actions, I was shocked and delighted to learn he had realized he handled the conversation in a way that was more hurtful than helpful and was open to listening to what I had to say about the potential consequences of having so much control over his kid's things. If a kid has made their decision to keep or let go of something, and it is continually not honored, there are potential long term consequences.

One, kids learn to not trust their own decisions, because they are being made to question them and they are given all sorts of reasons why their decision is not valid.

Two, they may resent the parents for not listening to their decision, and when they get older they may have what I call *'rebellion clutter.'* This is where they develop the attitude of it's my stuff and I can do what I want, when I want, and they will clutter and hoard just to spite their parents, without realizing they are hurting themselves in the process.

Three, they may want to get rid of something, but they have all sorts of background chatter that tells them why they should hold on to it, even if those reasons are not their own, which will cause negative attachment to their stuff and difficulties in letting go. I've shown you examples of that in my adult clients in this book. So, parents, if there is one piece of advice I can give you, that would be to let go of some of the control over your kids' stuff and let them have more of a say on what they keep and what they let go of. If you don't, your child will pay the price for it later in life. It will wreak havoc on their ability to make decisions, affect their relationships, their job, school, and many other areas of their lives. Remember, you were a child too once. There's a good chance that your own clutter and disorganization issues happened as result of beliefs, passed down through the generations, and drilled into you during childhood. Become aware of when you are imposing the beliefs about stuff you were taught as a kid on to your children, because those beliefs can potentially cause them to struggle with clutter and disorganization too. You have an opportunity to help your children create a healthy relationship with stuff so they don't have to grow up experiencing the stress that you have probably experienced as a result of disorganization and clutter.

So, before you react to your kids with a quick, "We can't throw it away because we might need it someday" or "we can't get rid of it because grandma might get mad if we do," stop and ask yourself if that is just a fear based belief that isn't really true. Even if it was, do you have to listen to it anymore? When do you get to have a say over your stuff?

If you can choose beliefs that are more relevant to who you want to be now and in the future, what you want out of life, and how you want to live, rather than living your life according to the "shoulds" other people are placing on you, then I would bet that you will feel more at ease and peaceful in your life.

Simply letting your kids have a choice in deciding when it's time to let something go will go a long way to helping them feel in control of their stuff rather than feeling controlled by their stuff. Empowering kids to trust their judgment will have a big impact on their ability to confidently and quickly make decisions. The faster someone can make and trust their decisions, the less of a struggle they will have with disorganization and clutter. Having your kid purge their things once every 3 to 6 months is an excellent way to exercise their decision making muscle and learn how to let go easily.

I started getting my daughter to purge her belongings at age two. At first, it was a bit of a struggle, but over time she has learned to make decisions quickly. Sure, there will be times when we disagree whether something should stay or go, but I do the best I can to respect her decision and trust that she will make the choice that's right for her when she's ready to.

Back to the action

As soon as her son left the garage, head down and noticeably upset, Leslie immediately questioned me on how I felt she handled her son's upset about the books. I advised her that his feelings needed to be acknowledged, even if she didn't agree with them. She then recalled how he expressed to her that since the divorce he didn't feel like anyone was paying attention to him, or listening to him anymore. I encouraged her to wait a few moments and then go to him and apologize for not listening to his feelings. This one situation alone opened the door to a whole new way of interacting with and understanding her kids. For her son, her approaching him to listen to his objections about books she had given away led to the opening of a proverbial Pandora's Box, and soon helped him express some pent up emotions. So much so, that a few days later she found him in his closet crying. When she asked him what was going on, he told her that between the move, the divorce, her declining health, and the organizing he was feeling overwhelmed and it was freaking him out. He told her he couldn't live like this anymore. That's when it finally hit her that living in a chaotic household situation was having a very negative impact not only on her, but her son too.

What's up with that?

I wasn't surprised to hear this. I have been on enough projects to know that organizing, purging, and moving things around inevitably starts stirring up dormant emotions for most everyone in the household. Clarity begins to happen as spaces get cleared and it reveals some hidden truths that someone may or may not want to acknowledge. That is why it's so important if you are going to get organized, that you have someone there to guide you through the roller coaster of emotions that most likely will surface. If you don't, those same emotions will stop you, and your project will more than likely go unfinished.

It can be somewhat compared to an addict going through a detox. Addicts often abuse drugs and alcohol as way to numb the emotional pain they may be feeling. When those vices are taken away, there is nothing but the raw emotion to deal with. For an addict, trying to deal with that on their own is extremely difficult, if not impossible. This is why they need to seek treatment from professionals who know how to work with their condition and guide them back to a healthy place where they are moving forward in their lives instead of relapsing. Successfully working through a clutter or disorganization problem can also require outside help because some situations require more drastic measures to be taken to help the sufferer.

Back to the action

As a result of becoming more sensitive to her own emotions, Leslie started becoming more sensitive to her children's emotions. She then began to question other ways she was interacting and dealing with them.

Together, we discovered that the way she was directing her sons to help her was not getting the cooperation she wanted and was creating a lot of tension between them all. I suggested that the source of tension may be partly to blame on a communication and processing issue. I explained that some people process information visually rather audibly. They need to see the information in front of them in order for it to stick and remember what to do. Writing tasks down will empower visual learners to get their tasks done faster, with less effort, stress, and overwhelm.

Using this technique, I advised her to write a list of small tasks and put it up in a place where the children could easily see it. For example, a list of chores such as: put clothes in the hamper, put toys back in the bin, vacuum the carpet, and make your bed.

By accommodating their learning style, I helped her to see that she would more than likely find her kids willing to listen to her more, which in the end would gain them all a higher level of cooperation.

This helped her to understand that she had a way of communicating that expected people to know what she wanted without her having to provide too much explanation. I have learned that operating this way tends to make the one expecting feel disappointed and frustrated because they will find more often than not people will not be able to meet their expectations and standards.

Keep it small and simple

Notice how I told Leslie to write a list of "small tasks?" By making a list with smaller specific tasks like "pick up your laundry," instead of tasks that are too big like "clean your room," you will get results from your kids that are more to your liking. Simply telling your child to go clean their room, unless they know exactly what you mean by that, is as effective as me telling you to go clean a room in your house when you have no idea what to do or where to start.

I can't tell you how many times I've been in someone's house and hear the parent shout at their kid to go clean their room. From there, the scene usually plays out with the parent becoming angry and distracted and then going back to what they were doing, while the child goes to their room upset and clueless as to where to start. To avoid getting in trouble, they make an attempt to clean, but become overwhelmed, mentally shut down, emotionally distracted, and wind up not finishing the job. Once their parent discovers they haven't met their cleaning expectations, which were never clearly defined in the first place, the parent becomes upset, blame it on laziness or deliberate misbehavior, and then the cycle repeats.

This may sound all too familiar to you or someone you know.

Exercise #1: Step into their shoes

In order to better understand how it can feel for your child when they need to clean their messy room, do this exercise.

1. Go stand in one of the rooms of your house that is messy and needs to be cleaned and/or organized.

2. Now tell yourself to start cleaning.

How did that make you feel? Did you notice feeling any anxiety or stress during this exercise? Did you feel yourself wanting to run away and do something else? Did you notice any other emotions coming up like fear, failure, disappointment, frustration, anger or overwhelm? Did you get started and shortly found yourself surrounded by piles of stuff and no clue where to put them? Well, guess what, chances are your kids are feeling the same way. If you weren't taught how to break things down into smaller steps, it makes sense you would experience difficulty getting things done too. Just like you, your kids need to be taught how to do it.

Exercise #2: Break it down

Do this exercise to help develop the skill of breaking projects and tasks down into smaller chunks.

1. Pick an activity that requires several steps to complete. For example, getting brakes fixed.

2. Now, use what I call the "forward thinking and backwards planning strategy," and think of the very last step that would need to happen in order to complete the activity.

3. From there, think of what immediate step needs to happen prior to doing that last step.

4. Keep thinking backwards of what needs to happen in order to do the next step until you figure out what is the step you can focus on first. The thought process might sound like this:

   "I have to get my brakes fixed."
   "If I want to get my brakes fixed then I have to find a repair shop."
   "In order to find a repair shop that is reliable and I can trust, I need to check out reviews of repair shops on Yelp."
   "In order to get on Yelp, I have to create an account."
   Creating a Yelp account would be the first step.

In this example, getting the brakes fixed isn't as simple as just getting in the car and driving to a random repair shop. By working on the step of creating the Yelp account first, the next step will be easier and then next thing you know the brakes will be fixed.

To build their planning and project management skills, I encourage you to sit down with your kids and apply the same exercise to one of their to do's needing several steps to complete.

Prepare for the task

Another roadblock to getting things done is not having what you need, when you need it, in order to complete the task. If you have asked your kid to pick up the trash in his room, but he doesn't have a trash can in his room then he may not complete the step, or it will require more effort to get it done, and take longer before he does do it.

Why not ask your kid what they need in order for them to do the tasks you are expecting to get done? Want them to hang their clothes? Maybe they need the closet rod lowered. Want them to make their bed, maybe it has to be moved away from the wall so they can easily get around it. Want them to keep their dirty clothes separate from their clean clothes? Get them two hampers: one for clean clothes, and one for dirty clothes.

Conveying the information in a way that works with their learning style, preparing in advance with the necessary resources to complete the task and breaking down tasks into bite sized tasks are invaluable skills to teach your kids which will have a huge positive impact on their lives in the future.

By teaching these fundamental skills, you will find your child becoming more cooperative, decrease the stress in the household, and equip them with the skills needed to live a thriving life instead of just surviving life.

Don't mess with the bald lady

After working with Leslie for only a few days, I had showed up for one of our sessions to discover she had completely shaved her head bald! You read that correctly, BALD. And you know what? She was rocking it Sinead O'Connor style. Apparently, the experience of shedding her emotional and physical stuff that no longer served her made her feel so free that she finally felt secure in shaving her head. Lyme disease had left her hair very unhealthy, and she had wanted to shave it for quite some time, however, every time she brought it up to her mother, her mom would belittle her and make comments that without her hair she would be ugly.

She was able to break free from the opinions and control her mom had on her to come to a place where she listened to what she felt was best for her, instead of what her mom thought was best for her. Many times before she had expressed to me that because of the control her mom had, she felt like she was, to use her own words, "just the supporting actor and not the lead actor in her own life."

Joseph, her son, wasn't so thrilled about the shave job. As a joke, when he saw her he started running up and down the street yelling, "Stranger danger, stranger danger," but in truth he was embarrassed to have her around his friends. She got an angrier reaction from her mom. Within two minutes of starting their phone conversation, they started to argue and she could sense her mom's disappointment oozing from the phone. It ended with her mom hastily hanging up after making disapproving statements like, "Why did you have to do something so drastic" and "why couldn't you cut your hair shoulder length?"

Her mother continued her angry rant for the next four days via text. Talk about having a difficult time letting something go!

But, Leslie, empowered in her new bald boldness, held her ground. Her reward for standing up for herself was that her hair started growing in stronger and healthier. After, she decided to go from black to blonde, the once negative comments she was getting from her sons got replaced with: "Your hair is legit, mom." MC Hammer couldn't have said it better himself.

The biggest breakthrough occurred when she decided to stand up to her landlord, once and for all. Her landlord had been very difficult to deal with for the whole year she had been living there.

A husband and wife team, the husband used his position in the FBI to intimidate Leslie, which up until then worked. She was repeatedly treated with disrespect, lack of care, and mistrust. Although she wanted to stand up for herself, she was afraid to rock the boat and jeopardize losing the roof over her and her children's head.

But once that hair came off, a whole new attitude emerged, and she wasn't going to take this intimidation any longer. She heard herself repeating the question asked earlier in the garage, "What is the worst thing that could happen?" Once she acknowledged her fears, she was able to move past them quicker, and instead listened to her gut warning her of the manipulative strategies they were using to try and cheat her out of her deposit. She understood that she was being given another opportunity to speak up for herself instead of continuing to be unheard and taken advantage of. Rather than let them complete the inspection after she left, she insisted she would be present and demanded the entire deposit be returned to her on move out day.

After several grueling conversations where, instead of crawling back into her cage, she chose to break through obstacles of condescending conversations, bullying, and pressuring. As a result she got her entire deposit check returned on the day she moved out. Not only that, but she found the courage to tell the FBI agent what a jerk he and his wife had been and that his status didn't scare her.

I feel like a proud mommy when my clients have empowered moments like these. It makes me want to get on a megaphone and shout, "You go girl." The moral of the story is if you need to get some cajones to state your boundaries, just do what Leslie and I called *"Going Britney"* and shave your head bald. Just make sure the paparazzi isn't around you when you do.

Stranger, Danger TAKE AWAYS

1. Always trying to be the type of person who tends to have a

save the world complex can lead to martyrdom, which can hurt the person trying to do the saving, and the ones they are trying to save.

2. Typically, where there is clutter there are unfinished projects which tie up physical, mental, emotional, and spiritual energy reserves, whether you are consciously or unconsciously paying attention to them.

3. Ask yourself a series of questions (listed earlier in this chapter) before you take on another project to make sure it's really worth tying up those precious energy reserves.

4. It's important to acknowledge someone's feelings even when you don't agree with them.

5. Going through the process of organizing tends to stir up emotions that may be difficult for someone to get through on their own. For this reason, seeking professional help is vital to the completion of your project.

6. Some people process information better visually than audibly. To increase cooperation and meeting your expectations, it would be helpful to write down what you want someone else to do instead of just speaking it.

7. Breaking tasks into small pieces will help you to get things done faster, easier and with less stress. Use the *forward thinking and backwards planning* strategy to decide what next actions are needed to complete a task.

8. Kids will grow up having a difficult time trusting their decisions if their parents always made them question their own judgment.

9. *"Rebellion clutter"* can happen when parents try to have too much control over their children's things and don't listen to the child when they make a decision whether to keep or let something go.

10. An adult may know it's time to let something go, but because of childhood programming from influential people in their lives, they may have a difficult time letting go of their things.

11. The amount of struggle one has with disorganization and clutter can be related to how quickly they make and trust their decisions.

.

"I have to keep this. This is my downstairs shirt."

Client Quote

Client with OCPD looks at wife's newly organized desk and says, "This is almost as good as sex."

Client Quote

"CHAOS: An acronym for 'Can't Have Anyone Over Syndrome'"

WordSpy Website

"Floordrobe: A noun, meaning a pile of discarded clothes on the floor of a person's room. (the word is a blend of floor and wardrobe)"

WordSpy Website

"People's homes are a reflection of their lives. It is no accident that people have a huge weight problem in this country, and clutter is the same thing. Homes are an orgy of consumption."

Peter Walsh

Stop Should'ing
All Over Yourself

Chapter 6

The client

When I decided to commit myself exclusively to my organizing business and work at it full time, I started looking for resources in my hometown of San Diego to promote me. I was interested in finding people who had a big influence and a large following. One such resource crossed my desk twice before I took notice, but boy did I hit the jackpot, on many levels, when I finally reached out to her.

Heather was a savvy, business woman, networking queen, and public relations genius who had her hand in many cookie jars. A wife and mother of two small children, she was running an up and coming company whose focus was helping other mothers. Like most mompreneurs I've met, we found ourselves emailing back and forth late at night when our kids were asleep and we could focus on getting our work done without interruptions.

I contacted her one day and simply said, "If you write a blog about me, I will spend a few hours organizing you for free." She was all over it and turns out it was perfect timing for her too. Like many of my clients, she had been thinking about getting organized for a long time but didn't take action on it. Having me show up in her life was the kick in the butt she needed to tackle years of clutter she knew one day she would have to face.

The assessment

From the moment we came face to face, there was an immediate bond. I was so grateful to meet another woman and mother who was also so passionate about her business, and I immediately considered her a trusted mentor in business.

The area needing organization was her desk in the office she shared with her husband, who also ran his own business out of the office. The desk was about 4-feet long with a couple drawers on both sides. On top of the desk was a large white hutch with ten cubbyholes that were crammed with all sorts of stuff. The drawers were even more jammed packed.

Though the office itself was also pretty full with stuff on the ground, in the corners, and on the walls, we decided to just concentrate on her primary workspace, her desk.

Heather's initial reaction to the estimate I gave her to sort, purge, and organize all the items in her desk and hutch was one of shock. Her first instinct was to think that I was ripping her off by way over quoting how long it would take. Then she realized I was doing it for free and began to trust me.

What's up with that?

One thing I always like to do with my clients before we start is to ask them how long they think it will take to organize their space(s). I do this as a way to check their reality levels. Commonly, I get an answer that is usually an underestimation of how long it will really take. If their reality levels are off, I have to set them straight by giving them a more realistic time frame. Underestimation is one of the main reasons why people typically don't finish their organizing projects.

At first many don't believe me when I tell them how long an organizing project will take, and some even get upset with me. It's only when we start digging in do they finally realize how much stuff they have and how extensive the process can actually be. This was the case with Heather.

Seeing how much stuff she had crammed, jammed, and piled

into her drawers, hutch cubbies, and on her desk confirmed my belief that you give someone who has cluttering tendencies a nook, a cranny, or any flat surface, and they are going to fill it, shove something in it, or put something on top of it. I lovingly refer to them as stuffers, topplers, pilers, fillers, crammers, and shovers. I have learned that people who clutter have a really tough time seeing empty space, and feel compelled to fill it right away.

For many, it actually makes them feel uncomfortable to leave a space empty. It happens almost every time that I remove something from a space, the client will look at me, biting their nails with the look of panic in their eyes and say, "So, what is going to go there now?" When I ask them, "Why does anything have to go there at all?" they usually look at me with this confused look on their face like I was speaking another language.

The idea of not filling every single space in their home is a totally new concept. For many, it brings up feelings of lack, sadness, and poverty. A previous client of mine had an adverse reaction when I removed all but a few knickknacks from her kitchen countertops. I was excited to bring her into the kitchen to show her my handy work and when I did the whole "ta da" bit I was expecting to hear the normal, "Oh my God, it's awesome," what I got was, "Oh, this makes me feel very sad." That was quite an eye opener for me. What I discovered in that moment is empty space = emptiness inside to a clutterer, and even more so to a hoarder.

Sometimes when I clear a space and it isn't immediately obvious what would be best to go into that space, I will suggest to the client that they leave it unoccupied for a period of about two weeks. I know it will be uncomfortable for them, but I also know it will help them to start to understand how strong their tendencies are to fill, fill, fill. Once their emotions calm down, they usually find they are able to be more rational deciding on what would be best to put in the space, rather than just filling it for the sake of filling it. Often when that happens, their choices end up creating a space that is more functional, comfortable, and esthetically pleasing.

Some clients can wait and some can't. Regardless, most of them do wind up gaining insight into how much of a grip their filling tendencies have on them, and then begin to modify their behavior to loosen the grip over time.

The change – the action

We must have sorted her items into categories that spanned at least thirty boxes. It was not only papers, but lots of small things. The smaller the items are the more tedious it can make the process. She was shocked at what came from this small area of her home, but understood right away the enormous impact it was having on her quality of life. She confessed that it was about fifteen years worth of accumulated stuff she had avoided dealing with.

Some of the stuff she was holding on to was her "should haves." Like her pile of everything she thought she "should" read, or the craft projects she "should" do with her kids.

We organized her desk to be more functional by only putting the items she really needed in her valuable real estate areas, and creating designated zones where items could be grouped together based on the similarity in how they are used rather than randomly thrown together.

Zone power

Grouping your items in to zones and defining it based on the activity the items in the zone are used for is one of the most effective ways of finding things easier, faster, and staying organized. For example, using a second drawer in your desk designated for office tools like a stapler, hole puncher, letter opener and scissors. This could be called the "office tools zone." Notepads, sticky notes, index cards and lined paper could all be grouped together and put in the "things to write on" zone.

Using this technique will help free up space in your mind because you'll have less places you'll have to remember to look for your stuff. It will also free up space in your home because you can contain similar items together using storage solutions like stackable, plastic bins that will give you the ability to fully utilize the vertical space.

After eight hours of work removing and sorting items from her desk, and putting back only what she needed, I bid her an adieu with the task of continuing to go through the boxes containing random items that didn't belong in her desk.

Exercise: Get Zoned

Pick an area of your home like your kitchen or office to group items into zones. Here are some ideas for zones you can use:

Office
Office tools
- Hole puncher, labeler, scissors, rulers, scissors
Electronics
- Computer accessories and software, cameras, video recorders, batteries
Office Supplies
- Paper, pens, pencils, erasers, highlighters, printer paper, labels, sticky notes
Kitchen
Baking
- Flour, cake mix, sugar, baking soda
Lunch
- Plastic cutlery, lunch bags, plastic storage containers, napkins
Entertaining
- Serving dishes and trays, fondue pot, place mats, table covers

Being able to find and put away your things easily, in my opinion is the highest priority goal of organizing. Getting zoned will not only help you accomplish this goal but will help you become more efficient, increase your confidence while using your space and bring a sense of peace and relaxation to your home and office.

The ah-ha's

During the process, Heather experienced many ah-ha moments. One of her biggest realizations was that she was unconsciously sabotaging her business.

She discovered she was feeling really guilty over the fact that, because her business had grown so quickly, she was now spending less time with her kids and more time on the business. As a result, she started unconsciously making her desk space more unmanageable and handling her tasks in a sloppy and inefficient way. She was self-sabotaging by setting herself up to implode within her business. This way if the business failed she could have a valid reason to go back to devoting more time to her kids. She also realized that by having and holding on to so much stuff she experienced a false sense of empowerment by creating an illusion of achievement.

What's up with that?

As I mentioned before, disorganization and clutter behavior is mostly an internal, sub-conscious issue. There are beliefs that are going round and round like a record player and serve as the captain steering the ship. It often takes another person to bring it to the disorganized person's attention in order for them to realize what they are doing and saying. That's why the work I do is so transforming; because I'm paying attention to the subconscious thoughts that come out of my client's mouth during their sessions that tell us what drives their clutter behavior.

There is just so much "shoulding" going on with cluttering. But just because you can doesn't mean you should. For example, just because you can scrapbook doesn't mean you should.

Side note: almost every time I work with someone who does scrapbooking, they almost always have clutter issues. Hmmmmm. Makes you think right?

Hanging on to all the shoulds takes up your precious internal energy reserves that could be used for all of the activities and projects that matter the most in the end. Guilt plays a ginormous role in disorganization and cluttering. I believe all guilt stems from fear. As I mentioned before, I also believe most clutter behavior stems from fear-based thinking.

It's not just "should" and "guilt" that causes clutter, it's our culture. We have been conditioned in America to believe the more stuff we have the more successful we are. That's called clever marketing folks. It was designed to get us to buy, buy, buy and attach our feelings of self worth to how much and what we own. Any person who has had a clutter issue and decides to let go of all that stuff will tell you that temporary feeling of gratification you get from buying stuff is usually not sustainable and, like Heather said, the stuff becomes more of a burden than an asset.

Does it serve you?

A year later, and after several rounds of continuing to purge the items from her desk and office on her own, Heather finally decided to tackle the attic she had postponed for years, again on her own. She still frequently emails me in total shock at how many more moments of insight she's had, and how she feels like she can breathe better.

When I worked with her, the question I asked her over and over again was "Does this serve you?" She continued to hear my voice long after I was gone and found she was always asking herself, "Does this serve me?" With that question alone, she has not only looked at her stuff in a different way, but her professional and personal relationships, as well. She's also looked at her value system and rearranged her social life to accommodate the person she wants to be rather than the person she thinks she should be. By clearing her space, Heather has found herself being more productive. With a more manageable work schedule, she felt ready to take on greater risks in her business, and has created a healthier work/life balance.

It's difficult to take on greater challenges with your business when you feel constantly buried. You may feel that any additional risks or opportunities that come your way will be the straw that breaks the camel's back and sends you spiraling out of control. Just think how much disorganization could be costing your business.

When should'ing stops

Her business and personal life has not only benefited from decluttering and getting organized, but so has her health. Heather decided to start dieting and exercising and has lost the weight she's been holding on to for years. Her biological physical clutter.

As she continues to go through and purge what no longer serves her, she continues to gain a deeper understanding of what works and doesn't work for her life and has made the connection how holding on to clutter has held her back from the quality of life she has allowed herself to be robbed of.

The weight – clutter connection

Speaking of weight, I've noticed that in many cases, there is a connection between clutter and weight issues. Clear your clutter and watch your motivation to get healthy and get in shape increase.

Along with being a Certified Professional Organizer, I am also a Certified Personal Trainer. I find a lot of similarities between getting in organizing shape and getting in physical shape. Both accumulating weight and accumulating clutter doesn't happen overnight. Getting rid of both also doesn't happen overnight. Both, more than likely started because of some un-serving belief that was probably created in childhood and learning to be organized is just like learning how to eat right and exercise.

You need to take on new habits and behaviors and get the right information. You need to set specific goals that are yours and not what someone else told you they should be. And both require consistency, commitment, and maintenance strategies that work with who you are, how you operate and your current lifestyle.

When you first learn how to exercise the correct way, your muscles will be sore and it will seem awkward. When you begin to learn how to get organized, your brain will feel sore, so to speak, and learning a new way of living and managing your life will also seem awkward at first.

But the good news is that although it may require more effort at the beginning of getting organized and starting an exercise program, after a while it will become more integrated into your way of being and will require less effort to maintain.

Doing the work to get there may not be easy, but I promise you the rewards will be worth all your blood, sweat, and tears. That, you can count on.

Stop should'ing all over yourself TAKE AWAYS

1. Sitting with an empty space tends to be very difficult to clutterers and hoarders because they perceive it as a feeling of emptiness inside themselves.

2. To gain a better understanding how strong your need to fill empty spaces may be, try living with an empty space in your home for a couple of weeks and see how it makes you feel. It could be just the corner of your bathroom sink or the top of your desk. Learn how to intentionally fill a space rather than just putting something there because an empty space makes you feel uncomfortable.

3. One of the reasons why projects tend to be left incomplete is because people underestimate how long it will take.

4. To make storing and retrieving your items faster and easier, establish zones where items are grouped together

based on their similarity in the function they perform.

5. Fear of failure, fear of success, and guilt are common reasons for self sabotaging behaviors leading to the unconscious cluttering of spaces.

6. Clutter consists of a lot of shoulds. And those shoulds take up valuable energy that can be used for the things that matter most in life.

7. Guilt plays a major role in clutter, which is a fear based emotion. It is my belief, that the majority of clutter is a result of fear-based thinking.

8. Many of your beliefs come from conditioning passed on to you through your family genealogy explaining why you may be having an unhealthy emotional attachment to stuff. Give yourself permission to examine those beliefs so you can consciously decide whether holding on to that belief will positively serve you at this time in your life.

9. Clever marketing tactics have created a culture in America where many people base their self worth on what and how much they own which can become more of a burden than an asset.

10. Clutter and weight issues often go hand in hand. There are similarities in getting into organizing shape and physical shape.

~ ~ ~ ~ ~ ~ ~ ~

"Awww that's the ashes of my ferret Phinny."

Client Quote

Chapter 7

Hiring the Right Professional Organizer

Congratulations for getting to this point in the book. I think many of us would agree that it's hard to find the time these days to sit down and read a book for even an hour a week. So here's a big cheerleader shout out

GOOOOOO YOU!

It's possible you stayed committed to finishing this book because something you read resonated at a deep level and compelled you to keep reading as though you knew there was a very important message in here for you. Some of you may have breezed right through and others may have read it sporadically. You may or may not have been ready to hear what I have to say. Either way is okay. Maybe now is not the time for you to hear it, but maybe now is the time when you must hear it.

I'm not a fast reader at all, however, I will occasionally pick up a book like *"Eat, Pray, Love"* or *"Getting Things Done,"* and just devour it. I choose to believe that my ability to read the book faster than what's typical for me was because, well, either I had a pretty heavily caffeinated drink that day, or I found that the information resonated with me on a deep level and it opened me up to a change that I was probably ready for. I have found that when I am open to change, the right information, circumstances, and people present themselves.

Did you find anyone's story sounding like your own? My hope is that you did connect with one of the stories and a new awareness was created for you. You don't know what you don't know. Sometimes it takes someone else to tell you or show you in order to be woken up and shown what you have been missing out on.

I have found that most of my clients have lived in the conditions of clutter for years and have adapted their whole way of living, operating, and being around it. They have strong emotional attachments to stuff and they finally opened their eyes one day and saw what it had done to their lives. I hear stories all the time that are riddled with remorse of what their lives have become and how different it is from what their lives use to be, or what they thought it would be.

It's pretty tough, if not impossible, to be living in America today and not have some sort of emotional attachment to stuff. I admit it, I still have one stuffed animal named Peaches that I have had since I was five. Sure, I've had to re-stuff him with paper towels and he has a missing eye, but at this point, I don't see myself ever getting rid of him. I'm way too attached to that darn thing. OMG! Did Miss Organized just say that? I sure did. Organizers have emotions too you know. Because I have developed a healthy relationship with stuff, I can feel okay about allowing myself to hold on to a few things that don't normally fit into all of my criteria of what to keep. It's kinda like when you've done pretty good sticking to your diet all week, and you allow yourself to have one cheat day. That's one of the 'bennies' of becoming organized and learning to have a healthier relationship with stuff.

I don't think there is anything wrong with having an emotional attachment to stuff, but when the attachment starts to have control over your life, and becomes a detriment to your well being then you have to start addressing the problem instead of continuing to ignore, minimize, and deny it. Now, if you stored in a memorabilia box that pair of tight, purple disco pants that remind you of your Solid Gold days, that is not a big deal. However, if you have 5 pairs of different colored tight disco pants in your closet that you dream of getting back into someday, then we need to talk.

At this point, you may be thinking to yourself that you want to get organized, and you know it would be good for you, but it seems like such a monumental task and you don't know where to start. Are you too embarrassed to ask for help? Maybe you are having a tough time financially and can't afford it. Both are reasons that prevented my clients from seeking help sooner, even when they really needed it. My solution to all of those concerns is easy. Start small.

See your home as projects within a project

You can't possibly organize an entire home all at once. You can't even organize an entire room all at once. In order to make the idea of getting organized less scary and more motivating, you have to break down your home organizing project into bite sized chunks. One room at a time, one space within the room at a time. Otherwise, it will seem too overwhelming, causing an inability to take action. This will only continue to postpone the satisfying feeling of getting to live in a clean and organized space, which feels pretty darn good, by the way. By chunking it down into mini projects, you will see results faster and feel more accomplished than if you were looking at the project from the whole house needs to be done now perspective. The more accomplished you feel during the project, the less frustrated you will become with the progress, and the more motivated you will be to continue getting organized.

Having difficulty asking for help?

Much like many of you, I too struggle at times with feeling like I have to wear the mask of "Miss Able" all the time. I've realized there comes a time when I have to raise the white flag, say I surrender, and ask for help.

Asking for help can be challenging for some of us, especially, if you have always been more of the independent type. We don't want to appear incapable. As if it's almost a blow to our ego that we can't do it all on our own, but the fact is that everyone needs help sometimes.

Help can come in many different ways. An extra hand, a cooked meal, kind words, honest feedback, a ride somewhere, watching the kids, someone who will listen, or just give you gas money. The trick is to come to know what your level of comfort in asking for help is and start asking from that place. Maybe you are not comfortable calling a Professional Organizer at this point, but maybe you can at least take a small step and call a friend to have a conversation about how your clutter has negatively impacted your life. Then after you have felt comfortable with that you can go online to a site like www.thecontainerstore.com and look at all the cool organizing products that you'll want to use when you are ready to get organized. Though it may be tempting to buy before starting the organizing process, I recommend you wait until you have figured out how much you need to store and where you will store it before buying anything. Otherwise, it may just become part of the clutter.

Conditioning yourself to receive help in even small ways can start to prepare you for accepting help in bigger ways. Chances are when you get there, you will be more willing to let someone come into your home and organize it.

The smaller the step, the more likely you'll do it. One of my favorite quotes is from a mystic philosopher of ancient China, Lao-Tzu. It echoes my point exactly: A journey of a thousand miles begins with a single step. Well said, Lao-Tzu.

But I can't afford to hire help

I believe in the idea that if someone wants something bad enough, they will find a way to get it. Consider this. It may not be so much that you can't afford to hire help, but it may be that your fears are stronger than your desire to take action towards getting organized. If the desire to get organized is strong enough, you will more than likely feel compelled to do whatever you have to do to afford help. I know because this is the state of mind most of my clients are in when they have finally contacted me. I often have them tell me that they will do whatever it takes to get organized and profess how desperate they are for relief from their clutter. This is usually because they waited so long to get help that now they are drowning in clutter rather than just wading in it. Once I had a client tell her husband she would sell her clothes if she had to in order to hire me. And you think I'm making this up?

The longer a space is left cluttered and disorganized the greater the chance for future clutter and disorganization. How do you stop that from happening and costing more time, money and energy to fix? Everybody say it with me, KEEP IT SMALL. Even if you have an entire house that needs to be organized, start with just a room. If hiring help for just a room is still unaffordable for you, then bring them in for at least 4 hours and let them get you started and show you how to do it on your own. Or maybe you can hire inexpensive help like a college student to deal with mundane tasks like filing and sorting papers. I have found that kids LOVE using the shredder. Why not pay your kids a few bucks to shred that growing pile of paper for you? How about finding a Professional Organizer who is willing to do a trade of services? I've traded services with people many times. I even traded services for the editing and design of this book. Thank you, Laura (www.writinginink.com) and Lisa (www.belladiadesign.com).

The bottom line is the most important thing you can do to get organized is to take some sort of action. Even a small step like getting a one hour consultation with a Professional Organizer would be a step in the right direction.

Start working on getting clear about why you want to get organized, be willing to take consistent action, decrease your tolerance towards a cluttered and disorganized home, increase your desire for an un-cluttered and organized home, and watch how you will be able to figure out a way to get the help you need.

Hiring a Professional Organizer

As a Professional Organizer with a hero complex, I wish I had magical powers to instantly transform everyone's homes into the feel good sanctuaries they are meant to be. Since I'm not able to do that yet, I'll give you some guidelines on how to hire the right Professional Organizer for you.

Choose the Professional Organizer whom you feel is right for you

Chances are you will have a lot more fun organizing and less resistance to the changes and advice if you worked with a Professional Organizer who you felt comfortable with. You should be able to tell upon the first phone call if the two of you will click or not. If your gut doesn't feel it's right than continue your search until you find one that makes you feel motivated, excited and secure in your decision to hire them and get organized.

Skilled in handling emotions

Organizing and de-cluttering can be quite the emotional roller coaster ride. Feelings like embarrassment, shame, guilt, anger, resentment, and fear will more than likely come to the surface during the process. Without a Professional Organizer experienced in guiding people through their emotions, you might wind up with a clean and organized home, but it will be more challenging to keep it that way because you didn't address the underlying emotions that contributed to it.

You may also get so emotionally triggered through the process that you will want to stop. An experienced Professional Organizer will help push you through those barriers and bring you to a place of understanding and willingness to keep going.

If it's important to you to learn how to deal with the emotions around your clutter then look for a Professional Organizer who understands the emotions that usually arise during a project and also can easily help navigate you through them.

Communication

When interviewing Professional Organizers, pay attention to the ones that you clearly and easily understand, and engages you in two way conversation that encourages you to communicate openly and honestly.

A good Professional Organizer will know the right questions to ask to understand your needs, which will help them to set up your environment in a way that will make the most sense for you.

The more open, honest, and direct the communication between you and your Professional Organizer is, the more personalized your experience will be, the easier it will feel getting through your project, and the greater chance of you successfully maintaining the organization.

Creative and resourceful

Although organizing may seem like a linear activity, most of the decisions that need to be made require a high degree of creativity and the ability to see several solutions that would best fit someone's budget, lifestyle, taste, and comfort level.

What color would look and feel best on the bedroom walls? Should the junk room be turned into an office or a guest room, or both? Would multi-colored versus standard colored hanging file folders make it easier to find your papers? Should an investment be made on one of my personal favorite shelving and container systems, The Elfa system, or just go with basic plastic bins?

These are some of the decisions that need to be made on an organizing project. Hiring a resourceful and creative Professional Organizer to make these decisions can not only save a lot of time, energy, and money, but leave you with a space that you will be happy with now and in the future.

To further promote the benefits of hiring a Professional Organizer, imagine this. Let's compare getting organized like going into war. In order to win a war the military has to have a plan in place or the chances of them winning the war are slim to none. They also need a leader who can see the enemy coming and knows the strategies and tactics it will use to derail the soldiers from claiming the territory and freedom they are fighting for. The soldiers also need to be properly trained to fight the war or their lives will be in jeopardy.

Think of a Professional Organizer like a colonel in the military and your organizing project like a war where there are lives and freedom at stake. Primarily yours! The Professional Organizer has the plan and the experience to conquer your clutter. The Professional Organizer also knows how to handle the beliefs, emotions, distractions, and excuses that will surface and try to derail you from completing your project, claim your territory and win your freedom. In other words, claiming your home and the freedom that comes with living in a clutter free space. A good Professional Organizer who will teach you how to get and stay organized could possibly teach you the very thing that can save your life from one that doesn't feel like living at all but merely existing. I don't know about you, but in my opinion, that's no way to live.

Hiring the right Professional Organizer, will be one of the best investments you will ever make. Guaranteed!

As with any consultant, you should also take a look at the consultant's website, see the photos they have posted of past projects, look at their credentials, and how long they have been in the profession. You want to make sure that the person you invite into your space and agree to pay will have the experience and talent to provide you with the guidance and support you need.

Hiring the right Professional Organizer TAKE AWAYS

1. You don't know what you don't know. Sometimes it takes someone else to tell you, show you or hold the mirror up to you in order to be woken up and shown what you need to see in order to make the changes to improve your life.

2. When you can learn how to have a healthy relationship with stuff, you can get away with occasionally holding on to something that doesn't fit within your established criteria for keeping things.

3. Emotional attachment to stuff becomes un-healthy when it starts to have control over your life and becomes a detriment to your well being.

4. The simple solution to most of the concerns around getting organized is to start small.

5. If someone wants something bad enough, they will usually find a way to get it, including hiring a Professional Organizer.

6. A good Professional Organizer will be someone who you feel comfortable with, is skilled at handling emotions, is an effective communicator that facilitates open, direct and honest communication and is creative and resourceful.

7. Imagine a Professional Organizer like a Colonel helping you fight the war on your clutter. They will have the plan and strategies to guide you through and train you to win the war on clutter and claim your freedom.

8. The more effort you invest in your organizing project, the more empowered, stronger and determined you will feel to do what you have to do to make sure it doesn't get cluttered and disorganized again.

"I make lists for my lists."

Client Quote

"I want to feel like I'm living in an adult space before an adult comes visits me."

Client Quote

"What you don't keep shells from Tahiti in your bedroom drawers?"

Client Quote

"Don't own so much clutter that you will be relieved to see your house catch fire."

Wendell Berry

"Take the first step in faith. You don't have to see the whole staircase, just take the first step."

Martin Luther King, Jr.

"Clutter is a physical manifestation of fear that cripples our ability to grow."

H.G. Chissell

Getting Started with Tracy's Tips

Chapter 8

Now that you have nearly finished this book and are hopefully uber-motivated to get started organizing, you are probably asking the big question, where do I start? Often times, it's this very question that causes people to avoid getting started at all because they have no answer. Or they start digging in without a plan only to find in a short time they wind up making a bigger mess than they started with. The new, bigger mess becomes overwhelming and either gets left there with the rest of the existing mess or gets crammed back into closets, cabinets, shelves, and drawers before guests arrive in a grand attempt to create the illusion of an organized space. This approach causes a lot of frustration and feelings of hopelessness that a clean and organized home will ever be possible.

Well, have no fear, Miss Organized is here with some simple tips to get you started and staying focused on your project instead of being like a deer caught in the headlights and getting frazzled during the process.

Getting started can be the hardest part of getting organized. Staying focused during the project can be as challenging. But once you do, you will quickly pick up momentum, endorphins will pump, getting rid of things will feel addicting, and you'll snap into a state of hyper-focus that will leave you wondering what the heck took you so long to get started. By following these simple tips, you will find the process less overwhelming, more manageable, and dare I say it, fun.

1. Choose a mini-project and create a detailed step-by-step plan

As I covered in chapter 5, the trick to getting through an organizing project faster and easier is to break your project down into mini-projects and small, bite sized tasks. Picking your clothes off the floor is a lot less daunting than the potentially overwhelming idea of cleaning your entire room. Organizing the sporting equipment in your garage can be done in hours instead of trying to organize the entire garage, which may take you days or weeks to complete. The less daunting and overwhelming a task is, the more motivated you will be to take action.

Though you may have an entire house that needs organizing, I recommend starting with only a room within your house to focus on. Even in that room, I recommend starting with a space in that room. Here are some examples of spaces within a room:

- The top of your nightstands
- The floor of your wardrobe closet
- Under the bed
- The top of your desk
- Your child's toy box
- Your jewelry box
- The coat closet

Once you have identified the spaces within a room you need to work on, write down the individual, mini-projects within that space, the tasks associated with completing the projects, and the estimated time to complete each task in each project. It might look like this:

Project: Book donations
Tasks:

1. Get bankers boxes at Staples – 1 hour

2. Purge books from bookcase and put in Bankers Boxes – 1 hour

3. Call library to see if they want donated books – 15 minutes

4. Load books into the car – 15 minutes

5. Schedule time in calendar to go to library – 5 minutes

6. Take books to the library – 1 hour

Writing down the estimated time to complete each task is crucial to the successful completion of your project. Most people severely underestimate how long it will take to complete a project and wind up not completing it at all out of sheer frustration it's not getting done as fast as they thought it would. My rule of thumb is however long you think it will take, double it. For instance, if you think it will take you 1 hour, plan on 2 hours.

2. Block out the project time on your calendar

It will not work if you say "I am going to organize my closet this weekend." You have to be specific as to what day and time frame you will be working on your closet on the weekend, otherwise the chances of you doing it are very slim. Then put the time in your calendar so you have a visual reminder of the commitment you have made. I recommend setting aside at least three hours to work on each mini project. Even if you only do the actual hands on work for an hour, you want to leave extra time to allow for potential distractions and temporary stopping points which will inevitably happen.

3. Have supplies on hand

For all organizing projects, I always have the following items by my side:

- Bankers Boxes (I recommend the 10 pack, Staples brand. Have 3, 10 packs on hand)
- Sticky notes to write a description of the box contents
- Black Sharpie
- Tape (to secure the sticky note to the box otherwise it may fall off)
- Large black trash bags for donations and trash

Make sure you have all the supplies ready before you start, otherwise you may get distracted by shiny metal objects on your way to find them while you are working on your project.

4. Eliminate distractions

When asked for advice on her best strategy for cleaning the house, my mom said, "Get everyone out of the house." There is a lot of truth in that statement. If the other household members have a habit of interrupting you when you are trying to focus (kids especially have an uncanny ability to know when you are trying to get your focus on), I highly recommend you ask them to either leave the house for a few hours or stay in their rooms so you can completely focus on what you are doing. Also, turn off your phone so you don't get de-railed by your gossipy friends, your demanding boss, your overly curious neighbor, your concerned mother and annoying telemarketers. It's best to also turn off other distractions like your TV and computer.

5. Get comfortable

I have found one of the easiest ways to stay completely focused on whatever I'm doing is to get comfortable before I start. I do this by appealing to all my senses. For example, eating something before I begin (peanut butter and apples are a great snack for staying grounded and focused), having a beverage on hand, turning on music, filling the air with something that smells good, adjusting the temperature to a comfortable setting, and wearing clothing I can easily move around in. Getting comfortable before you start will minimize the number of breaks you will feel the need to take during the process.

6. Get a good night's sleep and take vitamin C

Trying to de-clutter and organize when exhausted will make the process seem very difficult and make everything take twice as long. Do the best you can to get at least 8 hours of sleep for three days in a row before you start your project. Also, take vitamin C, or whatever supplements you typically take to stave off sickness before, during and after your project. Experience has proven, without fail, after a client and I organize and de-clutter, they get sick. Kicking up a lot of dust, releasing stuck energy, and emotional purging are big contributors to getting sick. So do yourself a favor and get as healthy as you most possibly can before you start. Your body, mind, and home will thank you for it.

7. Organize from the outside in

Though you may need to organize inside of your drawers, cabinets and shelves, it's often the stuff that is sitting on the outside of these areas that can cause a space to feel more overwhelming simply because it looks messier than if it was sitting inside of them. Whether it's on the ground or on top of a flat surface, creating clear space by first sorting the items you see sitting out into temporary boxes, will make the process feel less stressful and get done faster.

8. Organize while you organize

One of the most common mistakes people make while organizing is placing their stuff in scattered piles on the ground, cluttering up the walking space and creating what I call visual overwhelm. This tends to exacerbate the overwhelm they are already feeling and often causes the process to come to a grinding halt. To prevent this from happening, I recommend following these guidelines:

Use labeled containers with lids

- When grouping your things together, place them inside containers with lids, such as a bankers box and use a sticky note to label the contents of the box. This will help you to easily identify what the grouping of stuff is and stack the boxes against a wall to keep the walkways clear.

Go linear

- Keep the boxes or piles in a straight line rather than randomly placed throughout the space. This will also help to keep the walkways clear and make it easier to keep track of the stuff you are working with.

Create categorized sections

- Create sectioned areas where you put boxes with similar contents together into defined categories. Examples of categories are:
- Areas of the home such as living room, kitchen or garage
- Keep, throw away, give away and recycle
- By activity like sporting, entertaining or arts and crafts

9. Macro to micro sorting

When you first start sorting, define the items in the group by a general category name instead of a specific one. For example, sort all the items related to baking together and define the category as baking. Once you have done that, then you can go back and micro sort into more specific categories like flour, sugar, toppings, and mixes. Doing it this way, will make the process feel easier and go faster.

10. Acknowledge and treat yourself

One thing I commonly experience working with my clients is their tendency to focus on how much more work needs to be done rather than how much progress has been made. This self-defeating mindset causes the process to feel exhausting and uninspiring rather than invigorating and inspiring. I am always reminding them of the progress they have made and repeatedly tell them it's about progress and not perfection. It's important to acknowledge the progress you have made and then do something to reward yourself for your effort. Doing this will help keep you motivated and moving forward, even if it's only a little bit at a time.

Once you've accomplished something you are proud of, acknowledge yourself, tell someone, and maybe even treat yourself to something nice. Rewarding yourself is a good way of setting yourself up for a win on your next task however small or large.

You can do this!

I firmly believe the benefits that you will experience from getting organized will affect all areas of your life, and continue for the rest of your life. My big, audacious dream is that you will share and model that organized behavior for your children, family, friends, and co-workers to create a new way of being and put an end to this growing epidemic of cluttering so that we can restore the freedom we all crave, and the peace we all deserve.

Once you start to de-clutter and organize your space, you will have a greater understanding of the impact it's having on all areas of your life including your career, finances, health, and even your spirituality. Not to mention, the impact it's more than likely having on the relationship with your spouse, your children, your co-workers, your clients, your boss, and your friends and family.

You will realize the control it's had over the quality and direction of your life. The more effort you invest in your organizing project, the more empowered, stronger, and determined you will feel to do what you have to do to make sure it doesn't get that way again.

When the pain of living with clutter becomes greater than the pain of letting things go, you know that's a good indicator that you are ready to do something about it. When you can throw your hands up in the air, surrender, and admit you are no longer able to conquer your clutter on your own, help will magically appear.

If you are suffering with clutter and disorganization, I hope this book has shed some light on what is causing it. My desire is that I have motivated and inspired you to take action and finally do something about it, NOW! You can never truly understand how much better you will feel and how much more satisfying your life can be until you experience an organized home and life. Place the utmost importance on consciously creating a space where you are only surrounded by what serves you in a positive way and leaves you feeling good, healthy, and free. It's worth it. I promise. You can do this, one step at a time. Here's to your freedom.

~ ~ ~ ~ ~ ~ ~ ~

When talking about putting her desk in the corner, "Ok, we can put the desk in the corner, I just don't want to feel like I'm in time out."

Client Quote

"Oh that is my just in case Armageddon happens bin."

Client Quote

"Anyone who has ever cleaned out a closet and taken stuff to Goodwill knows how liberating it is. You feel lighter, your mind feels clearer."

Cecile Andrews

Chapter 9

Resources

Books

- *A.D.D. Friendly Ways to Organize Your Life* - Judith Kolberg
- *Organizing From the Inside Out* – Julie Morgenstern
- *Time Management from the Inside Out* – Julie Morgenstern
- *Women with Attention Deficit Disorder* - Sari Solden
- *Organizing The Disorganized Child* – Martin L. Kutscher and Marcella Moran
- *Growing Your Business!* – Mark LeBlanc
- *Clear Your Clutter with Feng Shui* – Karen Kingston
- *Eat That Frog!: 21 Great Ways to Stop Procrastinating and Get More Done in Less Time* – Brian Tracy
- *It's All Too Much* – Peter Walsh
- *Getting Things Done* – David Allen

My website

- www.missorganized.com

Additional Note:

Think about who you know who has also struggled with clutter and getting organized. Yes, we all know people like this because this is a common challenge. If you have benefitted from this book, consider telling others and/or giving copies as gifts. You can also refer them to my website at www.missorganized.com.

One of my favorite quotes:

"True stability results when presumed order and presumed disorder are balanced. A truly stable system expects the unexpected, is prepared to be disrupted, waits to be transformed."

Tom Robbins